A Champion's Guide to Growth Mindset

Develop Your Success Qualities and Achieve Your Goals. A Key to Resilience, Confidence, and Self-Discipline. Learn How to Stop Worrying and Turning Every Problem Into An Opportunity

Wayne Marshall Harrett

© Copyright 2022 - All rights reserved.

The content contained within this book may not be reproduced, duplicated or transmitted without direct written permission from the author or the publisher.

Under no circumstances will any blame or legal responsibility be held against the publisher, or author, for any damages, reparation, or monetary loss due to the information contained within this book, either directly or indirectly.

Legal Notice:

This book is copyright protected. It is only for personal use. You cannot amend, distribute, sell, use, quote or paraphrase any part, or the content within this book, without the consent of the author or publisher.

Disclaimer Notice:

Please note the information contained within this document is for educational and entertainment purposes only. All effort has been executed to present accurate, up to date, reliable, complete information. No warranties of any kind are declared or implied. Readers acknowledge that the author is not engaged in the rendering of legal, financial, medical or professional advice. The content within this book has been derived from various sources. Please consult a licensed professional before attempting any techniques outlined in this book.

By reading this document, the reader agrees that under no circumstances is the author responsible for any losses, direct or indirect, that are incurred as a result of the use of the information contained within this document, including, but not limited to, errors, omissions, or inaccuracies.

Table of Contents

INTRODUCTION 1

CHAPTER 1: IT'S ALL IN THE MIND 3

   THE RIGHT MINDSET 3
      What is a Growth Mindset? 4
      Benefits of a Growth Mindset 6
      Characteristics of a Growth Mindset 6
      Habits of a Growth Mindset 11
   BOXED IN 13
      What is a Fixed Mindset? 14
      Fixed vs. Growth Mindset 15
      How Mindsets Affect People 17
   YOUR THOUGHTS MATTER 18
      What is Positive Thinking? 18
      The Value of Having a Positive Mindset 20
      How to Adopt a Positive Mindset 21
   THE HEALTHIEST COMBINATION 23
      The Importance of a Healthy Mind and Body 24
      Tips on How to Maintain a Healthy Body and Mind 26

CHAPTER 2: WHAT'S THE PLAN? 33

   DISCOVERING ME 34
      Evaluating Your Sense of Self 35
      Factors That Can Impact Your Sense of Self 37
      Developing Your Sense of Self 40
   LASER FOCUS 43
      What is Goal Setting? 43
      Why is Setting Goals Important? 45
   GOAL-SETTING PRINCIPLES 46
      Five Goal-Setting Principles 46
      S.M.A.R.T Goals: The Golden Rule of Goal Setting 48

   Three Healthy Goal Categories...50
   Goal-Setting Outline 51
  TRUE TO YOURSELF...53
   What Skills Are Necessary?..53
   How Often Should We Review Our Goals? 55
   How Do We Achieve Goals?...56

CHAPTER 3: IN CONTROL OF ME 59

  WHAT IT TAKES 60
   What is Self-Discipline? 61
   Why Exercise Self-Discipline?...62
   Examples of Self-Discipline 62
  A FORTIFIED ME 63
   Eight Ways to Develop Extreme Self-Discipline 66
   Additional Tips For Self-Discipline..................................69
  LOST MY OOMPH 71
   Your Mind Is Always Directing You in The Right Direction 71
   Being Motivated Isn't Always Simple 72
   When There Is No Longer Any Motivation, How Do You Continue?..72

CHAPTER 4: THE WINNING FORMULA..................................75

  ON THE OFFENSE 76
   The Importance Of Strengths 77
   How to Identify and Use Your Strengths........................78
  ON THE DEFENSE 80
   Why Weaknesses Matter and How to Identify Them......80
   Turning Weaknesses Into Strengths 83
  BE ON GUARD..86
   How to Recognize The Intention of Others.....................86
   How to Protect Yourself From Those Who Want to Manipulate You 87

CHAPTER 5: LIFE IS UNPREDICTABLE 91

  THE GOING GETS TOUGH 91
   You Complain Nonstop...93
   Your Loved Ones Don't Make You Happy 94

You Hate Going to Work 95
You Put Unachieved Goals On Hold 96
You're Not Making The Most of Your Free Time 96
You're Not Acting in a Way That Honors Your Principles. 98
You're Doubting Yourself 99
THE TOUGH GET GOING 100
A Willingness to Consider All Options 101

CHAPTER 6: THE SKY IS NOT THE LIMIT 109

TURN UP THE NOTCH 110
How to Reach Your Full Potential 111
What Is Brain Plasticity and Why Is It So Crucial? 114
YOU'RE MY INSPIRATION 116
Learn From Others 116
Absorb Success 117
Envy Is Ineffective 118
CONSISTENT REBIRTH 118
Measure The Gain Rather Than The Gap 120
How to Track Your Progress 122

CHAPTER 7: A WORK-LIFE BALANCE 125

ON THE JOB 125
The Usefulness of a Growth Mindset to Professional Life 126
Self-Discipline and Professional Life 128
Nine Professionalism Characteristics 131
The Importance of Working Well With Others 134
YOUR INNER CIRCLE 136
Fixed Mindsets in Relationships 139
WATER AND OIL? 140
What Does Balancing Work and Life Mean? 141
Work-Life Balance Advantages 142
Accept That No Perfect Balance Exists 143

CHAPTER 8: SPEED BUMPS AND ROADBLOCKS 147

EVERYONE FAILS 147
Benefits of Failure 148
How to Accept Failure and Use It to Your Advantage.... 150

- Owning Up 152
  - Why Owning Your Mistakes Has Advantages 152
  - How to Accept Responsibility For Your Mistakes 153
- Spring In My Step 154
  - Acceptance's Healing Power 155
- Oh No! Not Again! 156
  - What Is Fear of Failing 157
  - Overcoming Fear of Failure (Step-By-Step) 157

CHAPTER 9: THERE'S ALWAYS SOMETHING NEW 161

- Willing to Learn 161
  - Take Development Courses 162
  - Use Web Resources 163
  - Attend Events 163
  - Online Networking 163
  - Get Certification or Further Your Education 164
  - Learn From Others 164
  - Read Case Studies and Research Papers 165
  - Read Widely 165
- Be Able to Take Criticism 165
  - What is Constructive Criticism? 165
  - Benefits of Constructive Criticism 166
  - Receiving Constructive Criticism 166
  - Destructive Criticism 168
- Out Of My Comfort Zone 170
  - Moving From The Comfort to The Growth Zone 171
  - Benefits of Leaving Your Comfort Zone 171
  - Seven Ways to Leave Your Comfort Zone 173

CHAPTER 10: THE DOMINO EFFECT 177

- Enough to Go Around 177
  - All Ships Are Lifted by a High Tide 179
- Passing The Baton 180
  - Engage 181
  - Educate 181
  - Equip 182
  - Encourage 182
  - Empower 182

- *Energize* *183*
- *Elevate* *183*
- BEING THE CHANGE 183
  - *Hope For Them* *184*
  - *Plan For It* *184*
  - *Share The Truth* *185*
  - *Act as a Model* *185*
  - *Disclose Yourself* *185*
  - *Challenge Them* *186*
  - *Ask Questions* *186*
  - *Invest Time in Them* *186*

CONCLUSION 189

GLOSSARY 192

REFERENCES 194

- IMAGE REFERENCES 203

Introduction

In an ever hectic and busy world, sometimes it can be hard to stop and ensure that our minds are guided in the right direction for growth. We might want to establish great accomplishments in life, but instead of going forward, we are stuck or stagnant, or maybe even going backwards. There is a better way, of course, but putting a foot forward and going for it might seem hard, or even so, impossible. But here's the truth. Our minds are all we need! It's that simple. By unlocking the amazing potential of our thoughts and embracing that it is our guide to this crazy and hectic life, we can achieve more than we even dreamt of.

In this book, I will share some of the best strategies to achieve a growth mindset, which will pave your way for a brighter future. You'll find practical tips and facts that are solely aimed to guide you in the direction of growth through the right mindset, even when there seems to be no way.

Over the years as a teacher and mental coach, I have established my confidence in the power of the right mindset to transform the course of a person's life, and my aim is to share this with you. I strongly believe in helping and empowering individuals to grow a positive mindset and enhance productivity in life. Due to my professional and personal experiences, this has always been my aim, because I am certain that there is a lifetime of opportunities just waiting to be snatched up, and all you need is the right mindset. My goal is to share this with you.

This quick read will show you how to understand and manipulate your mind to think in a positive and productive way, not only for now, but for a lifetime. Then, you will learn how to apply the strategies to your everyday life.

The objective, in the end, is to help you reap the best of your potential, using the very key that you have had all along: Your mind. Wanting to achieve remarkable accomplishments isn't as far-fetched as we might think, and by the end of this book, you will know exactly how to achieve this.

Your life, future and goals are in your hands. It might seem like a lot, and of course, there will be others along the way to help you. But in the end, your success is entirely dependent on what you do, how you do it, and your thoughts toward it. Have you ever heard someone tell themselves that they can't do something because they don't *think* they can? Perhaps you have even had this thought as well. Then, as a result, those very thoughts prevented them from achieving or completing the task. Why? Because their mindset wasn't in the right place.

So take the step to establishing the growth mindset of a champion by using the techniques and guidance of this book. Your future self will thank you for it.

Chapter 1:

It's All in The Mind

Can our beliefs about who we are and what we are capable of influence how we live? Absolutely. The way we perceive our intelligence and abilities has an impact on how we feel, but it can also have an impact on our performance, our ability to form new habits, and our ability to learn new skills. People who have a growth-driven mindset are better equipped to achieve the lives they desire.

If you have a growth mindset, you think you can improve your skills and intelligence through time. The way we think holds a significant amount of power no matter if we are students, members of the working class, or both. Hence, we should understand how this works.

The Right Mindset

Our intrinsic beliefs in the flexibility of human qualities are known as mindsets. Having a 'right' or 'wrong' mindset might seem like a blurred line for many people. But maybe it's time to equalize the mentality.

Although some people equate concepts like 'grit' and 'effort' with a growth mindset, this is not always so. Effort is required, it is not the only factor. Your mindset has much more to do with your ability to access your toolbox of problem-solving techniques than it does with your effort. Your effort serves as a tool, not as a goal in itself. So, when fostering growth mindsets, it's crucial to recognize improvement.

What is a Growth Mindset?

A growth mindset is characterized as a notion that intelligence is flexible and developable. With a growth mindset, intelligence, and talent are seen as traits that can be improved with practice.

This isn't to say that those who adopt a growth mindset automatically believe they have the potential to succeed. There are still limits to what any of us can accomplish. People who have a growth mindset simply think that they can get smarter and more talented by working hard and doing things.

Individuals that have a growth mindset are more likely to use a mastery approach to learning, welcome difficulties, and put forth effort to learn. For instance, growth-minded people view task failures as an essential component of learning and "bounce back" by stepping up their motivating effort.

Growth-minded learners frequently value lifelong learning and the satisfaction of modest personal development. Furthermore, they do not consider their intelligence or personalities to be fixed characteristics. Without being intimidated by the prospect of failure, they will harness their learning resources.

A growth mindset is essential for learning, perseverance, motivation, and performance since it views 'failings' as temporary and adaptable. It increases your likelihood of:

- Being open to lifelong learning.
- Believing that intellect can be raised.
- Increasing your effort to learn.
- Believing hard work leads to mastery.
- Considering setbacks to be only temporary failures.
- Considering criticism as a source of knowledge.
- Eagerly accepting challenges.

- Taking inspiration from other people's accomplishments.

- Considering criticism as a chance to gain knowledge.

Benefits of a Growth Mindset

A growth mindset has a positive impact on motivation and academic achievement. Additional benefits of having a growth mindset are:

- Decreased burnout.

- Less mental health issues like anxiety and sadness.

- Decreased behavioral issues.

Characteristics of a Growth Mindset

Some of the most significant figures in human history have demonstrated how their growth mindsets enabled them to achieve their ultimate accomplishment. They become more powerful when they adopt a growth mindset and push themselves to go above what is expected of them.

Develop the characteristics of a person with a growth mindset in order to achieve change and success. It will help you to learn how to accomplish your mission more quickly and easily!

Here is a list of ten qualities that every individual with a growth mindset possesses or works to improve in order to succeed in both their personal and professional lives.

A Love of Learning

People that have a growth mindset are eager to learn new things. Your objective should be to increase your skills as much as you can. Your ambition to learn shouldn't wane, whether you are working as an FBI agent or in a position with less responsibility.

Your ultimate objective should be to become proficient in your abilities and view each new day as an opportunity to broaden your knowledge and pick up new skills. You view it as a chance to strengthen yourself and get rid of any deficiencies you might have.

Self-Belief

One of the most important traits is self-confidence. In actuality, those that adopt a growth mindset truly believe in themselves. You will have the confidence that you will succeed in overcoming any difficulties or hurdles you face. You'll understand your purpose once you have mastered these obstacles or trials. You'll also learn more and gain more experience as a result. You will be able to persevere thanks to your faith and confidence in yourself.

Estimated Risks

One important factor is the risk-reward scenario. If you never take a chance, you don't think you'll be in a better position. Instead, you should think that taking chances while acknowledging the possibility of failure is preferable.

Maintain Momentum

People that have a growth mindset think that living in the present is important. Nothing can be done to change the past; it is what it is. Therefore, those who have a growth mindset are able to learn and develop. Don't worry about the past; instead, concentrate on the here and now, which will benefit you in the future.

When you have a growth mindset, you believe you can accomplish something because you are aware that the current moment is all there is for life. You also believe that the past should remain in the past. Being in the now is a crucial aspect of growth.

Actions Matter

Even though they have huge dreams, people who start small tend to perform at their best. They realize that they need a place to start, but they can then move on. The idea behind their actions and deeds is to improve their consciousness, which they are aware is not sufficient in and of itself, by using their growth mindset.

They can improve their knowledge through action, and it is this deliberate repetition that gives them success.

Naturally, acting can start at any point in life; some people begin acting in high school, while others begin acting in their later years. The primary element that promotes this quality is that the person steps outside of their comfort zone.

Take on Interesting Challenges

An individual who has a growth mindset welcomes challenges. You should actually view a challenge as a chance to improve yourself. When the chance to challenge yourself presents itself, seize it, and demonstrate how a positive mindset may lead to success.

You will get wiser and stronger as a result. Challenges can occasionally be frightening, but you may not know how you will respond until you actually face the problem. People that have a growth mentality think they can conquer any obstacle and come out the other side stronger. This should be your aim.

Self-Disciplined

Those with a growth mindset think differently from other people. They understand that in order to be successful and get what they desire, they must put in the necessary effort. They have a high level of self-control.

You should be able to fully concentrate on the end result because of your devotion. As a result, you will achieve and reach your goals thanks to your tireless efforts and tenacity. You don't waste time showing you can; instead, you move beyond your foundational knowledge and, with a positive outlook, you find a successful way.

Surrounded With Positivity

Being optimistic is a quality shared by persons with a growth mindset, which is one of the qualities associated with being a highly effective person. They undoubtedly go through trying and stressful moments, but their optimism helps them develop stronger, fresh attitudes that help them comprehend what positivity is all about. Success is something that results from positivity. You must have a growth mindset if you want to advance and accomplish goals.

Supporting Others

Successful people sometimes underestimate the value of giving back. Everyone requires assistance from someone at some point in order to realize how crucial it is to assist others. They learn from this that skills may be developed with a little direction and assistance. This way of thinking is supported by the idea that in order to achieve your goals, you must first assist others. As a result, your daily objective should be to assist others because doing so frequently allows you to profit more than you gave.

Greater Resistance

One of the main characteristics of the growth mindset is resilience. Growth is not a process that takes place instantly. It takes time to develop. Successful people are aware that it is not simple to be successful. This indicates that they are fully committed to achieving their objectives.

Whether or not you occasionally stay on your tracks, you won't stop until you reach the opposite side of the mountain. You can continue on your path to success and advancement in this way.

Habits of a Growth Mindset

Habits are instinctive actions that we do every day. Habits can be developed with time, consistency, and effort. However, those who have a growth mindset may exhibit certain habits that we should aim to develop as well. Here are five habits of growth minded people.

Resisting Negativity

Be careful not to let criticism sidetrack or demotivate you. While constructive criticism can be beneficial, it's equally crucial to cultivate and pay attention to your own inner, growth-minded voice. Determine whether the criticism you get, both from yourself and others, stems from a fixed perspective or from a growing mindset. When coaching yourself to develop this habit, think about how you would support a friend or coworker who was starting a new learning experience.

Believing in a Successful Outcome

The marshmallow test, the most well-known willpower experiment created by psychologist Walter Mischel, demonstrated the importance of being able to concentrate on the good feelings you will have after achieving your objective (Dutton, 2015). This skill is essential for success. Create an image in your mind of what success would look like. Maintain a sharp focus on your intended result and picture how amazing you will feel once you have perfected your new talent or ability.

Accepting New Challenges With Open Arms

It is possible to learn new talents and abilities through tackling challenging activities. The opportunity to learn new skills and make new synaptic connections presented by challenging or novel tasks can increase your performance over time.

Celebrating Your Accomplishments

Your drive to attempt new things, persist, and reach your potential is directly influenced by your confidence in your talents. The habit of spending some time celebrating and acknowledging your accomplishments is vital. Recognizing the effort that has helped you master a new skill or achieve success in a current area of interest. Remember past successes that required learning, and remind yourself that having a growth mindset helped you succeed, as you start a new learning curve.

Being Receptive to Fresh Insights and Experiences

A fixed perspective actually turns off our ability to learn. Those with a growth perspective continue to have active brains and learn more than those with a fixed mindset. It is crucial to keep an open mind to new experiences and knowledge because when we do, our neurons fire and connect, helping us to enhance our skills and talents with a growth mindset.

Boxed In

Can our beliefs about who we are and what we are capable of influence how we live? Absolutely. The way we perceive our intelligence and abilities has an impact on how we feel, but it can also have an impact on our performance, our ability to form new habits, and our ability to learn new skills.

If you have a growth mindset, you think you can improve your skills and intelligence through time. If you have a fixed mindset, you can think that your IQ is fixed and that you will never be good at something.

What is a Fixed Mindset?

People who have a fixed mindset think that traits like talent and intelligence are fixed; they think that they are born with the degree of intelligence and natural skills they will have when they are adults.

A person with a fixed mindset typically shies away from obstacles in life, quits easily, and feels frightened or intimidated by other people's success. This is due in part to a fixed attitude, which believes that intelligence and talent are things that you 'are' rather than something you can grow.

Negative thinking can result from fixed attitudes. For instance, someone with a fixed mindset can struggle with a task and think that their lack of intelligence is to blame. A growth-minded individual, however, may struggle with the same activity and think they need to practice more.

People who have a fixed mindset feel that certain characteristics cannot change, regardless of how hard you try, and are more prone to:

- Believing that talent and intelligence are constant.

- Avoiding obstacles to prevent failure.

- Ignoring the opinions of others.

- Feeling frightened by other people's success.

- Covering up imperfections to avoid criticism from others.
- Thinking their efforts are in vain.
- Considering criticism as personal.
- Quitting easily.

Fixed vs. Growth Mindset

The human brain is always changing and evolving, contrary to what science originally claimed, which was that it stops growing in childhood. Our 'software' can be updated through learning since many different regions of the brain react to experiences.

Some individuals still believe that you are limited to the skills and 'smarts' you were born with, despite the neurobiological facts. The concept of fixed and growth mindsets was first investigated by Stanford University psychologist Carol Dweck (Smith, 2022).

In her key work, Dr. Dweck outlined the two basic ways that individuals categorize intelligence or talent as either being

- **A fixed mindset**: One that holds people's intelligence to be fixed and static.
- **A growth mindset**: One that holds that intelligence and skills can be developed with work and education.

The usual belief of those with a fixed mindset is that their intelligence level and skills are innate. However, those who have a growth mindset recognize that not understanding something or not being excellent at it can be a transient situation, so they don't need to feel bad about it or want to outdo their present level of intelligence.

To better explain this difference, take for instance, a scenario where a school teacher selects two of her students to participate in the debating tournament, although they both have not had any experience with debating. The students with a growth mindset would be willing and excited to take on the challenge, and take the opportunity to learn and expand their knowledge of debating.

On the other hand, the student with a fixed mindset will doubt themselves, believing that there is no possible way they can do this without looking or appearing knowledgeable.

Mindsets are domain-specific and fall on a spectrum between the fixed and growing extremes. A student might, for instance, have a growth mentality when learning to code yet a fixed attitude when it comes to public speaking. Even within a specific field, a person might initially tackle a particular difficulty by working hard and asking for assistance—displaying a growth mentality—but may later interpret losses as a sign of low intrinsic ability—underscoring a fixed attitude.

How Mindsets Affect People

While individuals with fixed mindsets can achieve success when their studies or aspirations are progressing well, a fixed-mindset approach can be detrimental to them when they are faced with significant setbacks. People who have a fixed mindset may interpret failure as an innate inability to get better at a difficult task, which can lead them to feel inferior (also known as "imposter syndrome") and incapable of succeeding (resulting in a loss of self-efficacy), drop out of a course, major, or educational experience, and/or give up learning skills that could be useful for academic and professional growth.

In essence, we know that having a growth mindset is more beneficial than having a fixed one. Do you have a fixed mindset? Consider these questions to assess if you do:

- Do you often shy away from hard situations, or hesitate to take on a task that you are not sure of the final result?

- Are you easily discouraged by setbacks and criticism?

- Do you readily seek new opportunities and are eager to learn new things?

If your answers were 'yes' for the first two and 'no' for the last, then you are leaning in the direction of a fixed mindset. If you answered 'no' for the first two and 'yes' for the last, you are more in the line of a growth mindset.

Although it might not be easy to change from a fixed to a growth mindset, acknowledging that you do is the first step.

Your Thoughts Matter

At one point in our lives, we might've heard that our thoughts matter the most. But what if I told you that there is a foundation of truth behind it? How we think is the first step to determining our trajectory in life. So, if you have positive thoughts towards your life, others or a situation, you will reap the benefits of these thoughts. Hut if you think negatively against the former, the results will be just as negative.

Hence, in this section, we will discuss the importance of positive thoughts in everyday life and how you might build these positive habits.

What is Positive Thinking?

Positive cognitions, in general, can be regarded as positive thinking. This separates the power of positive thinking from feelings, our actions, and longer-term effects like happiness or depression. A person's level of optimism, self-esteem, and life satisfaction are all signs that they were practicing positive thinking. While it is true that these ideas include positive thinking, they are frequently viewed as potential benefits of positive thinking techniques.

The acronym THINKING makes it simple to remember the following eight essential skills that support positive thinking:

- **T**ransforming negative thoughts into positive one.

- **H**ighlighting the situation's positive elements.

- **I**nterrupting negative thoughts by using distraction and relaxation techniques.

- **N**oting the necessity of using optimistic thoughts.

- **K**nowing how to divide a task into manageable portions.

- **I**nitiating hopeful assumptions about each aspect of the issue.

- **N**urturing approaches to combating negative thinking.

- **G**enerating one's negative thoughts to produce happy feelings.

You'll see that this list contains both cognitive and non-cognitive strategies, such as relaxation.

According to Davis (2020), positive thinking can be seen as a construct with four dimensions:

- **Self-affirming thinking**: This includes thoughts of being one's own biggest fan.

- **Self-assertive thinking**: This encompasses ideas of serving people well.

- **Self-instructive and analytical thinking**: This involves the ideas that direct action.

- **Self-reflective thinking**: This entails thinking confidently.

Positive thinking covers a wide range of thinking techniques and strategies, which in turn should improve well-being.

The Value of Having a Positive Mindset

The advantages of each type of positive thinking may vary because it has various definitions and elements.

First, it's generally beneficial for well-being to think positively about yourself. You will have a greater chance to succeed and achieve, for instance, when you believe in your capacity to do so. Stress decreases by our tendency to regard ourselves more favorably. This information mostly agrees with studies on self-worth, self-confidence, and self-esteem, which are seen to be examples of positive thinking (Davis, 2020). Therefore, people who think positively frequently feel happier, interact with others more positively, and handle stress better.

Additionally, positive thinking gives us a challenge-oriented mindset, that is, the opposite of shaving a fixed mindset. When we approach issues with a challenge mindset, we think we can handle the difficulties at hand. So, we benefit more from the challenge perspective, when we think we have greater control.

How to Adopt a Positive Mindset

Just like almost every aspect of life, it's easier said than done. So, what are some illustrations of positive thinking then? Let's dissect this in more detail.

Past-Oriented Positive Thinking

Negative or pessimistic thinking about the past may make issues worse. We can get over unpleasant things that have happened in the past by changing these thoughts to more positive ones.

Here are some examples of past-oriented optimistic ideas that acknowledge the challenging situation while casting a favorable light on the past:

- "I gave it my best effort."
- "Even if the presentation didn't go well, I did learn what to do better the next time."

- "I know my childhood wasn't ideal, but my parents did the best they could, and I will be better now."

Present-Oriented Positive Thinking

Present-oriented positive thinking can help us manage our problems more skillfully, relieve stress, and possibly enhance life pleasure while living in the moment. Here are a few examples of present-oriented positive thoughts:

- "I'm very grateful to have friends and family who genuinely care about me."

- "That nap was very relaxing. I'm happy I took it."

- "I always try my best, but I might make mistakes, and that's okay."

Future-Oriented Positive Thinking

Negative or pessimistic future-focused thinking may cause more concern or anxiety. Positive thought changes can help us become more present and stop us from feeling bad about things that haven't even happened yet. Here are a few examples of positive forward-looking ideas:

- "Everything will work out just fine."

- "I'm very excited to attend the meeting next week."

- "I'll keep working for my dreams, so I'm confident in a bright future."

Positive thinking can be used to address various negative thought patterns and perhaps enhance a number of wellbeing-related factors by focusing on the past, present, and future.

The Healthiest Combination

There are many ups and downs in life. Daily life events have an ongoing impact on our mental and physical health. So, in this section, we should discuss the importance of keeping our bodies and minds in good shape, and how we might do this.

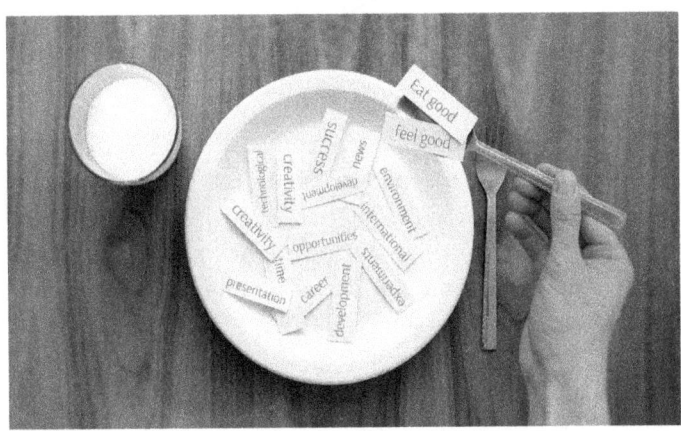

The Importance of a Healthy Mind and Body

The difficulties we face on a daily basis, which have an impact on our health and mental stability, are easy to overlook. But we must fight back and make every effort to adopt healthy lives, which will provide us with both healthy bodies and brains. There are a number of benefits of good physical and mental health. Here are the most essential.

Better Daily Habits

Your entire quality of life will likely be considerably greater if you have a healthy body and mind. Our energy levels will undoubtedly increase if we routinely exercise, meditate, or engage in self-care practices. We can perform tasks quickly and more contentedly when we have more energy and are in good physical and mental health.

Enhanced Sleep

The fact that maintaining strong physical and mental health would have a significant impact on sleep quality is a key factor. A good night's sleep is invaluable, and you will be able to get a good night's sleep quite easily and naturally if you are in good physical and mental condition.

Mental Clarity

A healthy mind and body complement one another. And when we reach that healthy connectivity, our thoughts are clear, enabling us to think and act in a healthy way throughout our daily lives.

Sometimes, mental clarity simply refers to a person's capacity for relaxation. One benefit of having a healthy body and brain is being able to take time for yourself and clear your mind occasionally.

Reaching Goals

People who have both physically strong bodies and clear, healthy brains typically advance in life more than anyone else. The ability to accomplish goals is made possible by having that all-encompassing power in body and soul.

People who are mentally and physically well have better careers, greater success, and use creativity to reach their objectives. Being healthy generally is crucial for those who wish to realize their goals, regardless of whether they are career-related or not.

Better sleep and a clearer head might also help them relax or make important decisions. More importantly, being in good physical and mental health allows us to easily fulfill our life goals and maintain a positive outlook.

Tips on How to Maintain a Healthy Body and Mind

A healthier future may result from the lifestyle decisions you make today. The right mindset is aided by every component of health both mentally and physically. We know the importance, and now, we'll find out how. First, we will talk about some ways to improve your physical health, then, we will talk about maintaining a healthy mind.

Have Good Physical Health

Maintaining both your physical and emotional wellness can have a lasting impact on your body. It is simple to skip the healthy choices when there are so many quick, easy-to-eat meals or unhealthy snacks accessible. To maintain a high level of energy and remain active throughout the day, try to follow a "three meal schedule." Drink a lot of water to stay hydrated and keep your metabolism running.

Observe Your Drinking

While many people use caffeine and alcohol to elevate their mood, the effects are only fleeting. Some people drink to delay the emergence of negative emotions or to mask underlying feelings of anxiety or depression.

However, your mental and physical health may be significantly impacted as the initial feelings of energy or excitement after drinking diminish. This is extremely risky because it has the potential to worsen already existing conditions or cause long-term health issues. Try to limit your daily alcohol consumption to three to four units, or none at all. Also, avoid drinking anything with caffeine after seven o'clock at night.

Eating Right

Healthy eating habits don't have to be difficult to establish and keep up. You may significantly alter your eating pattern and establish lasting, healthy eating habits if you start by implementing little changes into your everyday routines. By adding one new objective each week, try to incorporate at least eight of the ten following goals into your diet:

- Eat fruits and vegetables every day.
- Aim to eat half of your grains as whole grains.
- Switch to low-fat (1%) or fat-free milk.
- Pick a range of lean protein-rich foods.
- Compare the amount of sodium in various foods.
- Drink water instead of sweetened beverages.
- Eat some seafood.
- Reduce your intake of solid fats such as cookies, cakes.
- Prepare and eat healthy snacks.

- Control your portion sizes.

Exercise

The benefits of daily exercise—both physical and mental—are numerous. Your body releases endorphins during exercise, which can significantly lift your mood. To get some exercise, you don't need to spend a lot of money or join a gym; simply walking or biking to your destination, cleaning your house while listening to music, or gardening are all inexpensive and effective methods. Once you get used to it, you'll discover that things get easier to do and that you look better, which will improve your self-esteem. On most or all days of the week, try to get some exercise for at least 30 minutes.

Maintain a Healthy Mind

It's easy to fall off track with your mindset when things get a little overbearing, or you simply get distracted. However, here are a few effective tips to help you maintain a healthy mindset.

Speaking With Others

Keeping in touch with friends and family is now simpler than ever in the modern world. Being able to relate to others is a crucial aspect of what makes us human, and neglecting this aspect of life can have a negative impact on your mental health. Maintaining solid relationships and staying in touch with others can aid in or even prevent the development of many mental health issues, which have communication-related roots. If you're having trouble, your friends or family may be able to help you the most. So talk to them about how you feel and pay attention to what they have to say.

To Change The Scenery

We occasionally find ourselves in a rut. An excellent approach to unwind, elevate your attitude, and explore more of the world is to go on vacation or take a break away from your natural environment. Not all of us, however, can take off for the sun anytime we feel like it. However, there are a lot easier (and less expensive) methods to take a vacation from the daily grind that can do just as much to enhance your mental health. Your mind will learn new things and adapt to new conditions by taking a different route to work or school, or just changing the arrangement of your furniture.

Start a Hobby

These days, work pressure consumes such a large portion of our life that we sometimes forget what we enjoy. Perhaps you enjoy painting, playing an instrument, or have always wanted to make some DIY accessories. By giving yourself some alone time, you may express yourself, concentrate, and manage your stress. When you express your emotions through a poem, song, or painting, you can better comprehend how you are feeling and feel better.

Recognizing Your Individuality

Many people compare themselves unjustly to those they see on social media or on television because they are unhappy with how they look, how they speak, or what their background is. These emotions may result in an ingrained sense of unworthiness or even bring on illnesses like depression or an eating disorder. This, of course, is not an ideal mindset to have. Speaking with others and expressing your emotions will help you have a better knowledge of your strengths and flaws. If you believe that doing so is helpful, set aside five minutes each day to write down one positive and one bad characteristic about yourself. Then, attempt to accept the fact that you are the best version of yourself that you can be.

Respect For Others

It comes naturally to care for other people, no matter who they are. Returning caring for people who show you care is a crucial component of maintaining strong relationships. Simply signing a "get well" card at work or calling an older relative to see how they're doing could accomplish this. Genuinely caring for others can significantly enhance your healthy mind and provide you the chance to explore emotions you may have lost touch with. You can better comprehend why people care about you and why you should take care of yourself if you allow yourself to feel emotions for other people.

Challenge Your Mind

Your brain needs exercise to remain healthy, just like the rest of your body. You can accomplish this in a variety of ways, including playing computer games and crossword puzzles. Try figuring out the numbers in your head first, then see if you were right mechanically, rather than immediately working out your costs using a calculator. Another effective technique to ensure that your memory remains in top condition as you age and in daily life is to learn a new word every day. Since your mind is your most precious instrument, maintaining its optimal functionality is crucial to maintaining happiness and leading a complete life. Challenging your mind is also a key component of having a growth mindset.

Chapter 2:

What's The Plan?

Knowing who you are and what motivates you gives you a sense of self. This is important, because understanding your values, and purpose in life will help guide you, your goals, and inevitably shape the type of mindset that you have. Setting goals and sticking to them are what sets the growth mindset-driven person on the right track.

In this chapter, we will discuss finding your sense of self, making goals that are in line with a growth mindset and knowing how to stick to them.

Discovering Me

Your impression of your qualities or characteristics is referred to as your sense of self.

Your self-image or distinct identity as a person is shaped by your personality traits, skills, likes, and dislikes, as well as your beliefs and moral principles. People who have a clear sense of who they are tend to be able to describe these components of their identity with ease. If you have trouble naming more than a few of these qualities, it may indicate that your sense of self is less clear.

Even if you don't give your identity much conscious thought, it still has an impact on how you live. Knowing who you are enables you to lead a purposeful life and create fulfilling connections, both of which can support overall emotional well-being and build the foundation of what your mindset is like.

However, some people can succeed in life without divulging too much about who they are. So, you might be wondering: Does having a strong sense of self really matter?

It absolutely does.

Having a strong sense of who we are helps us make decisions in life. Knowing what originates from our own selves versus what originates from others enables us to live genuinely, whether it is with regard to smaller things like favorite foods or bigger issues like personal values.

Recognition of your own value can also be fueled by your self-image. Although you aren't flawless (because who is?), you are still very valuable.

Understanding who you are as a whole, including the qualities you're proud of and those you'd like to develop, makes it simpler to accept who you are and build a growth mindset. When you have a good sense of your nature and abilities, you'll find it easier to address any areas where you do feel unsatisfied with yourself.

On the other side, it can frequently be challenging to know exactly what you desire when you don't have a strong sense of who you are. When it comes time to make significant decisions, you might find it difficult to make any decision at all if you feel unsure or indecisive.

As a result, rather than moving forward with your own momentum, you can merely drift through life. Even when nothing appears to be amiss and you are unable to pinpoint the cause of your sadness, this frequently results in discontent.

Evaluating Your Sense of Self

Where on the spectrum does your sense of self fall?

You may have observed a tendency to make decisions based on what you believe others desire from you. Or perhaps you lack numerous goals or strong passions and are glad to simply go with the flow. Is this the mindset you would like to have? Is this really a growth mindset? But do you know if you even have this outlook on your sense of self?

The following questions can help you gain some understanding:

- **Do I say yes to everything to satisfy other people?**

    While occasionally making accommodations for others is entirely acceptable, if you usually go along with their requests, you probably aren't living for yourself. It may indicate a less-developed sense of self if you define yourself primarily through your interactions with others or your capacity to please your loved ones.

- **What do I do well?**

    Knowing and believing in your skills to use your strengths to accomplish your goals are essential components of having a strong sense of self. A strong sense of self is frequently a sign that you have a good hold on your abilities and are using them to their fullest in everyday life.

- **What makes me joyful?**

    What aids in your relaxation and enjoyment? What leisures or pursuits give life meaning? Finding the people and interests in your life that are important to you and that you wouldn't want to lose or change might reveal a lot about you.

- **What values do I hold? Do I act in accordance with that?**

    Your sense of self can be greatly shaped by being aware of your particular ideals. Values are the qualities you value most in yourself or others, such as empathy, honesty, reliability, kindness, and so forth.

- **Do my decisions align with my interests or those of others?**

    If you're unsure of how to respond to this question, consider it from a different perspective: Would you make the same decisions if you were alone? Strong sense of self is often shown in decisions that are primarily driven by your aspirations and objectives for yourself.

Factors That Can Impact Your Sense of Self

Let's say that you had some difficulty responding to the questions above.

You may be wondering, perhaps in some distress, "Who am I, really?"

You might feel more at ease knowing that having a hazy sense of self is not at all unusual. This doesn't imply that you did anything wrong or that you'll be stuck without a distinct identity for the rest of your life.

It will be easier for you to start honing your self-image if you have a greater awareness of the factors that contribute to its formation.

Individuation

The process of individuation, or creating a distinct self, starts in early life. Children require space to explore, learn, and convey needs and preferences in order to properly individuate. We can build a strong sense of ourselves when we are allowed to show our characteristics without feeling guilty or ashamed.

You might react by ignoring your inner sense of self if your efforts at self-expression only receive criticism or reprimands from your loved ones, friends, or anybody else. Remaking yourself into someone who is more likable could seem safer and more advantageous. But being true to who you are without apologies will help you build your sense of self.

Attachment

Your attitude in adult love relationships as well as how you develop your identity can be impacted by an insecure attachment.

Attachment problems can be rather complex. You might change your behavior to win your friend's approval if you don't feel confident in their love and acceptance. The compliments and love that follow serve to support the idea that the best (and even the only) way to succeed in relationships is to shape your behavior after that of others.

This process typically repeats itself in your subsequent relationships as you suppress your own wants in order to satisfy those of your partners or friends because you believe that this is the only way to keep their devotion.

An Attempt to Fit In

It would have been simpler for you to adopt the persona of a social chameleon if you had trouble fitting in with your peers when you were a teenager. Instead of clinging to your sense of self, you started changing who you were to fit in with more than one group. Acceptance is an effective motivator. This lesson can stick with you well into adulthood if your adaptable sense of self serves you well throughout your teenage years.

At work, with your family, and while you're with friends, you might adopt one identity; at home, another. It can be challenging to discover your genuine nature and stressful for you to alternate between these many 'selves.'

Developing Your Sense of Self

You may feel hollow and unfulfilled if your sense of self is unstable, but it's always possible to improve it. To start creating a more distinct identity for a growth mindset, try these tactics.

Define Your Values

A fundamental component of identity are personal values and beliefs.

Your belief system can help you identify what is most important to you and establish your position on significant issues. For instance, your desire to uphold animal rights may influence your decision to buy products that don't test on animals and to eat foods that you know more about.

Your personal limits with other people can be influenced by your values. For instance, if you value honesty, you can be clear that you can't continue to be friends with someone who lies to you.

While you don't have to pinpoint every one of your beliefs at once, try to consider a few as you go about your day and engage with others.

Choose Your Own Actions

Most of the time, you should make choices that are primarily for your health and wellbeing. You should also consider your partner's or your kids' needs if you have them, but you shouldn't put yourself last.

Keep in mind that when your needs are not satisfied, you are less able to help others. You may have previously allowed others to decide on crucial matters for you, such as your education, employment, or where you live. If so, it could feel awkward, even scary, to begin making choices for yourself.

But it's okay to start out modestly. Practice acting without seeking advice from others and do it only because you want to. Remember that asking for advice from others does not imply that you lack self-confidence. Speaking with dependable family members about challenging choices is completely healthy. At the end of the day, it's crucial to make the choice that's right for you, despite their thoughts.

Get Some Alone Time

Spending time with someone is how you get to know them, isn't it? Therefore, spending time by yourself will be necessary to get to know yourself better. Even though it may seem strange at first, taking some time away from your partner or family is healthy.

You can make any use of this time. If you want to maximize self-discovery, try these things:

- Discovering new interests.
- Volunteering.

- Taking up reading.
- Meditating.
- Maintaining a journal.

Think About How to Fulfill Your Ideals

According to research, discrepancies between your ideal self (who you imagine yourself to be) and your true self (who you actually are) might contribute to feelings of discontent and even despair (Raypole, 2020). Your ideal self is who you picture yourself to be.

In other words, even while it's a really good start, understanding who you are might not be enough. Your emotional wellbeing may suffer if you don't respect this feeling of self.

Once your sense of self is more clearly defined, think about what you can do to make your life more consistent with who you are. You might, for instance, consider what adjustments you can make to your social or professional contacts with people.

It might be challenging to understand what it means to be 'self,' in part because your identity evolves as you learn and develop throughout your life. It's normal to experience occasional periods of uncertainty or self-doubt. If you frequently feel unfulfilled or find it difficult to identify your needs and wants, you might want to give some self-discovery some thought.

Laser Focus

Do you ever have the feeling that you are just drifting through life without really knowing what you want?

Perhaps you are completely clear on your goals but are unsure of how to get there.

Setting goals fits into this situation. Setting goals is the first step in making a future plan, and they are crucial for the growth of skills in all areas of life, from work to relationships and everything else in between. They are the object of our metaphorical arrow.

Success is paved with an understanding of the value of objectives and the methods involved in setting them.

What is Goal Setting?

Setting goals is an effective motivator, the importance of which has been acknowledged in numerous therapeutic and practical settings for more than 35 years (Houston, 2019).

The purpose or intent of an action, such as achieving a particular competence level within a given time frame, is known as a goal. They represent the degree of skill that we aspire to achieve and serve as a helpful framework for evaluating our present performance.

Goal setting is the method by which we reach these goals. Every person's life depends on the process of picking goals to pursue; if you remain motionless, you won't thrive as a human being. The significance of the goal-setting procedure should not be undervalued.

The foundation of the Goal-Setting Theory is the idea that conscious goals influence behavior and that fully functioning human behavior is directed and controlled by personal objectives (Houston, 2019). To put it simply, we must choose what is best for our personal wellbeing and then set goals to accomplish it.

So, why do some people work harder than others to complete tasks? The Goal-Setting Theory takes a first-level approach to the problem of motivation; it places focus on a direct degree of explanation of individual differences in task performance. Individuals must be motivated if their skills and knowledge are comparable.

According to the theory, different performance goals are the easiest and most direct motivational explanation for why some people perform better than others, suggesting that defining and modifying goals can have a big impact on performance.

Why is Setting Goals Important?

Goals have an impact on how strongly we feel and act; the harder and more important the goal, the stronger our efforts will be to reach it, and the greater success we will feel once we do.

Success experiences and the good feelings it brings help us gain self-assurance and faith in our skills. According to research, goal setting drives the hunt for fresh methods to boost performance (Houston, 2019). Finding new methods to use our knowledge and stretch our talents improves task-relevant knowledge while boosting self-effectiveness and self-assurance.

Setting goals entails making future plans. Positivity about the future helps us set goals and take into account the steps necessary to reach them. Planning skills enhance our sense of control over future events and target outcomes. Setting and achieving goals can also encourage the growth of our intellect and mindset.

Goal-Setting Principles

Initial theoretical statements about goal setting determined how intended and actual achievement compared. When a person has precise goals to fulfill, their performance is better than without them. Having clear goals improves performance.

In the 1990s, goal setting research led to the theory of goal setting and task performance, which recommended five important criteria for successful goal achievement.

Five Goal-Setting Principles

Goal setting doesn't just happen like that. There are layers to it that entails what true goal setting is. Below are the five principles that make up goal setting.

Commitment

Commitment is a person's attachment to a goal and resolve to attain it, despite challenges. Commitment and difficulty boost goal performance. Given their devotion to a goal, if they do poorly, they will likely increase their effort or adjust their plan to reach it.

Less commitment to goals, especially tough ones, increases the likelihood of quitting. Strong commitment increases the likelihood of achieving goals and performing as planned. Several things affect our dedication including, perceived goal, desirability, and capacity to achieve it. Whether defining a goal for yourself or others, you must have the passion and knowledge to acknowledge it.

Clarity

Specific goals direct you, while vague goals lack motivation. Goal clarity increased motivation and job satisfaction.

Set implicit, clear, measurable goals. Clear goals help you understand the task at hand. You know what's needed, and your success motivates you.

Challenging

Goals should be difficult yet attainable. Challenging goals can enhance performance by increasing self-satisfaction and motivation to push our abilities to the maximum. This is also a significant component of a growth mindset.

Unachievable goals cause discontent and frustration. Hence, achievement and its anticipation motivate us. The truth is, if we believe we can achieve a tough objective, we're more likely to finish it.

Complexity

Overly difficult tasks add demands that might mitigate the benefits of goal setting. Goals that are too difficult for us to accomplish can become overwhelming and have a bad effect on our motivation, productivity, and attitude.

Realistic time frames should be used for such objectives. A goal can be reassessed for difficulty with enough time to complete it, while also reviewing and improving performance. If the task's complexity exceeds their capabilities, even the most driven individuals may lose interest.

Feedback

Feedback improves goal setting. Feedback, including internal feedback, helps determine how well an objective is being reached.

Additionally, clear and straightforward feedback enables essential action. Feedback helps us set new, more attainable objectives if we fall short of a goal's benchmark. When feedback is delayed, we can't assess the effectiveness of our strategies, slowing growth. Therefore, when we believe we're making enough progress, we can learn new skills and set more ambitious goals.

S.M.A.R.T Goals: The Golden Rule of Goal Setting

While reading about healthy goal setting, you may question if there's a widely accepted method.

The S.M.A.R.T methodology helps you develop skills-based, timely, measurable goals. The S.M.A.R.T framework provides a sense-check for goal setting if you're unsure. It is as follows:

- **S is For Specific**: Clearly define your aims. This can be the difference between understanding what you want and how to attain it and being frustrated by an open-ended goal. "What, why, where, when, and how" might help you develop specific goals. For example, if you want to run a marathon, you can ask the questions: What's the route? When was this goal due?

- **M is For Measurable**: Having a quantifiable goal makes tracking progress easier. How does one know when they've reached peak fitness? We could run forever without knowing if we've reached our goal. Changing the objective to "I want to get fit so I can run a full marathon" makes it more explicit and allows for continual progress monitoring.

- **A is For Achievable**: Is your objective realistic? Humans are hardworking, imaginative organisms with great potential, but we must establish realistic goals or risk being disappointed. If you've never exercised or have impaired lower-body mobility, it would be absurd to say, "I'll run an ultra-marathon by next week." Finding a balance between work and difficulty can be hard, but goal achievement must be worth the effort.

- **R is For Relevant**: We emphasize the subjective 'why' here. Does your aim come from internal or external pressure? Would a marathon fulfill you? Would you enjoy reaching your goal or be disappointed?

- **T is For Time-specific**: Deadlines optimize goal benefit versus time. Saying, "I'll run a full marathon by summer's end" is a clear, attainable goal.

Three Healthy Goal Categories

We can classify goals into three categories when setting them. By doing this, we can establish a goal for each category or a number of goals for a single category, allowing us to concentrate on one or more areas that need special attention.

Time Goals

Goals can be divided into short-term and long-term categories. Short-term goals, as the name implies, are easier to accomplish than long-term ones. While there isn't a clear cut criterion to distinguish between a short-term and long-term goal, we can think of goals that take a day to a few weeks to complete as short-term goals and objectives that should take a month or more as long-term goals.

Focus Goals

Focus goals are significant, life-changing goals. These are long-term goals that may require many adjustments.

For example, the goal, "I will read fifty self-help books by the end of next year" may need creative reading timelines, assessment of your budgets and adjusting your schedule to enable enough time to meet the deadline.

Topic-Based Goals

These goals fit one area of your life. Personal, career, or financial objectives might be topic-based.

A financial goal would be "To save $1,000 by the end of the year" while a personal aim could be "To lose X amount of weight within six months."

Goal-Setting Outline

Personal goal setting is something only you can do. This outline will help you set and achieve personal goals.

Be Progressive

While enthusiasm is wonderful, don't rush into making goals too quickly. By reducing the amount of goals you set, you'll be less overwhelmed. Setting a few basic goals will help you get started while avoiding failure's negative emotions.

As you attain your goals, establish longer-term challenges to push your abilities. After setting goals, evaluate them often. When making goals, it may be helpful to check your progress daily or weekly.

Focus on Short-Term Goals

Set short-term, realistic goals first. Setting short-term objectives, such as "I'll learn to make lasagna next week," allows for more frequent goal reviews and recognition. More frequent accomplishment increases pleasant emotions and drive to set new short-, medium-, and long-term goals.

Make Them Positive

Reframe negative goals like "I want to quit eating junk food" as "I want to feel healthy and will improve my diet." The original motivation for negative objectives frequently stems from a negative place, for instance, "I want to quit eating so much unhealthy food because I feel unattractive." These negative implications might cause demotivation and self-criticism.

True to Yourself

Once we've learned how to set goals and start working towards them, whether personal, professional or financial, it's our job to ensure that we stay true to ourselves and maintain these goals. It is important that, as we aim for our goals and develop a growth mindset, we stay motivated, consistent, and accountable for our mistakes.

What Skills Are Necessary?

For successful goal setting and achievement, there are a few fundamental skills needed. The excellent thing is that they can be developed through practice and learned. It's probable that one or more of these factors are at fault if you are unable to reach your goals or achieve your driven mindset.

Planning

The proverb "fail to plan, plan to fail" applies to achieving successful goals. Poor planning has an adverse effect on performance in regard to goals. Planning and organizing skills are essential to achieving goals. Planning effectively allows us to prioritize tasks, keep our attention on them, and avoid unimportant distractions that can cause us to lose sight of our ultimate objective.

Self-Motivation

Our efforts to set goals will be unsuccessful if we don't have the motivation to accomplish them. Motivation to succeed pushes us to learn new strategies and abilities in order to get what we want. The desire to persevere under more trying conditions is a significant factor in achieving goals.

Time-Management

Goal setting is only one of the many areas of life where time management is useful. While most people believe that setting goals is a particular time management practice, time management is equally necessary in order to achieve a goal. We are doomed to failure if we do not carefully examine the amount of time needed to achieve a goal.

Additionally, the amount of time we devote to goal setting strongly affects task performance; the longer we spend at the planning stage, the more probable it is that we will be successful.

Flexibility

It's inevitable that things won't go according to plan at some point. To achieve your goal, you must have the adaptability to overcome obstacles and the endurance to maintain your efforts in the face of difficulty.

Self-Regulation

To advance your own social and personal objectives, you should learn to control and manage your own emotions. The capacity to effectively consider and express motivational goals, aims, and missions results from developed emotional intelligence.

Confidence and Attention

Setting objectives won't work if we're not dedicated to achieving them. Goals must be significant and applicable to us personally, and we must be certain that we can achieve them or, at the very least, make significant progress toward them.

How Often Should We Review Our Goals?

Once goals are set, reassess them. Reviewing goals helps measure progress and ensure they're still relevant.

Some goals can be accomplished quickly, but others require patience and motivation. Reviewing goals depends on the goal itself. Hence, you should regularly review them.

If you've set smaller milestones on the way to your end goal, revisit them weekly. Knowing your progress allows you to adjust your behaviors and goals so as not to undo your hard work. Regular reviews enable you to reflect on the complexity of the goals you've set. Is it difficult? How can you improve?

frequent goal reviews also ensure the aim is still relevant—is this what you want? If you don't 'check in' on your progress, you may lose focus of your ultimate goal, resulting in disappointment, frustration, and decreased enthusiasm to achieve it.

How Do We Achieve Goals?

Have you ever made a New Year's resolution only to abandon it by mid-January? You probably set a too-general, too-ambitious, or half-hearted aim. Healthy goal setting can help with these challenges.

Write Down Goals

Writing things down may seem needless, yet it's helpful. Write out your goals and plan your path. Writing things down enhances recollection, and having a physical reminder means you can review it at any moment.

Review Your Plan Often

Consider your goal's timeline. If your goal is difficult, split it into smaller, more doable goals. Instead of declaring "I want a promotion," commit to taking on a new project in four weeks. Ensure your decision is right.

Specifics and Progress Checks Are Key

How we frame goals affects our success. Specific goals are better than general ones. Rethink your goals, then expand on them.

Reward Your Triumphs, But Don't Punish Failures

When you reach a healthy eating goal, give yourself an internal pat on the back. Recognize and enjoy your success. Being resilient is crucial. When necessary, reevaluate your goals, and make changes. Goal setting is about what you are able to realistically achieve, not what you aspire to achieve.

Chapter 3:

In Control Of Me

To achieve most things in life—including success and happiness—people need self-discipline. Self-discipline prevents you from overindulging in unhealthy snacks after deciding to eat healthier food, or it prevents you from spending hours on end binge watching your favorite TV show after knowing you have a project to work on. Everyone has a distinct definition of self-discipline and self-control; some of us may find it easier than others to exercise restraint. Everyone, however, may learn to develop their self-control 'muscles,' since it is also vital in establishing a positive, effective growth mindset.

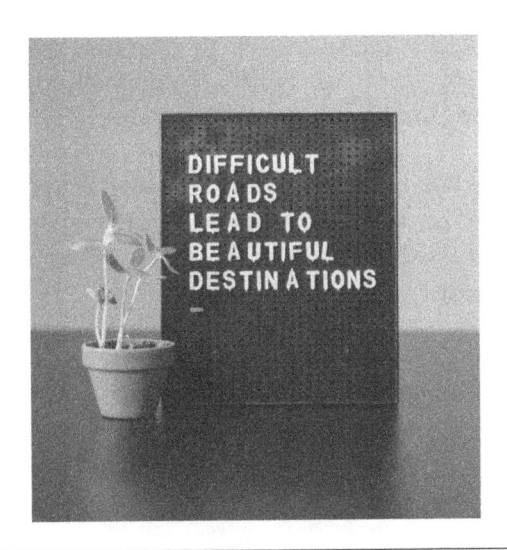

This chapter will discuss self-discipline, how to develop and maintain it, and how to apply it to achieve your goals for a growth mindset.

What It Takes

Hypothetically, speaking, every morning before the sun comes up, Angela gets up to work out. She works very well at the office, putting high-value projects first and ignoring distractions. She attends an online session in the evening and will receive her PHD in a few months.

How is it that people like Angela continuously do so much? And how might we make such strides in both our personal and professional lives? The key to the solution is self-discipline working together with your mindset. This is what motivates us to carry out our noble intentions and objectives, despite any reluctance. If we are disciplined, we may postpone momentary pleasure (or put up with momentary trouble or discomfort) in order to pursue long-term gain.

Self-discipline is crucial because of this. In this section, we'll look at what self-discipline actually is, why it's important, and how it works with self-regulation to achieve goals.

What is Self-Discipline?

In general, self-discipline is described as conscious control that is directed toward achieving goals by removing barriers or impediments. It is the capacity to restrain prepotent responses in support of a higher objective, and making such a decision involves intentional effort rather than being automatic.

Examples of self-discipline in the context of work might include getting up and going to work on time, paying attention in a meeting rather than daydreaming or scrolling through social media, making a choice to do work on a project over watching a TV show, or completing challenging tasks despite boredom and frustration.

Self-discipline is the capacity to move forward, maintain motivation, and act despite any physical or mental discomfort. You demonstrate it when you consciously decide to work toward improving yourself, even in the face of obstacles like diversions, difficulty, or bad circumstances.

Self-Discipline vs. Self-Regulation

Self-regulation is not self-discipline. Self-discipline inhibits strong impulses while self-regulation reduces their frequency and severity by controlling stress and stress-recovery. Self-regulation allows self-discipline to take place, and the reason is brain-based.

Why Exercise Self-Discipline?

Self-discipline is beneficial in many aspects of our lives.

For example, it motivates you to produce excellent work even when you do not even feel like it. Even if you're ready to give up, it provides you the courage to maintain your professionalism with those you work with, even clients. It aids in your perseverance and achievement of the objectives you set for yourself. You can achieve great success through self-discipline even when the odds seem overwhelming to others.

This important realization is consistent with the goal of self-discipline, which is to achieve control over your ideas and habits so that they serve you rather than the other way around.

Examples of Self-Discipline

The multiple processes that make up self-discipline include preparation, self-monitoring, and persistent effort. Having self-discipline is a crucial life skill that affects a variety of things, including:

- **Healthy routines**: Your physical and mental well-being will greatly benefit from having the self-discipline to get adequate sleep, a healthy diet, and give up unhealthy habits like smoking.

- **Work**: Self-discipline is crucial for job and professional success since it helps you stay focused on achieving your objectives, no matter how big or small.

- **Managing money**: Being financially disciplined is a necessary component of making sensible judgments.

- **Emotion control**: When you develop self-discipline, you put forth the effort to express your feelings in constructive ways and develop coping mechanisms for difficult circumstances or setbacks.

- **Time management**: Applying self-discipline to time management is perhaps one of the hardest things to achieve in our society. However, developing good time management skills can help both your professional and personal life.

A Fortified Me

Self-discipline is a skill that anyone may develop. Although it could take a lot of work and your patience and kindness toward yourself may be tested, it is not impossible. You could start practicing self-discipline in the following ways:

- **Be mindful**: You make choices every day that affect your lifestyle, such as what to eat, when you should go to bed, or whether to send that passive-aggressive text. Temptations are something we can resist or give in to. For instance, perhaps you shouldn't buy groceries when you're hungry. Why? Because you are more prone to purchase snacks, high-calorie foods, and other less nutrient-dense foods. You can exercise self-discipline by resisting the urge to eat unhealthy foods when you're hungry or by forgoing the urge altogether. To make great changes in your life, it's crucial to be conscious of what works for you and constantly use those methods.

- **Find your 'why' or the reason why you want to do something**: Finding your 'why' will make it easier to figure out your 'how.' When you find your 'why,' or the reason you desire to accomplish a task, you can reassure yourself when things become difficult.

- **Make a plan**: If you want to increase good habits and decrease bad habits or acquire a new skill, developing a detailed plan will assist you to get to whichever your definition of success is. If you don't know where you're going, it may be easier to get derailed. If this applies to you, you can construct an outline of clear actionable steps you plan to take on a weekly or daily basis until you achieve your objective.

- **Start small**: Now that you have a plan, take a step, take a small step. Don't try to do everything in one week since this might leave you feeling overwhelmed and may even lead you to quit your goal.

- **Resist temptations**: In psychology, there is a theory called "ego depletion," which emphasizes that willpower is a limited resource and that we only have a finite 'reservoir' of mental resources to endure temptations (Hagan, 2016). Every day, you use your self-discipline to resist temptations until the 'reservoir' runs out. For instance, if you're resisting drinking three beers, removing temptations can significantly increase the likelihood that you'll reach a successful outcome.

- **Try time blocking**: The Pomodoro technique, very popular among busy students, recommends that you should break up your work time as follows: work undisturbed for 25 minutes and then take a 5-minute break—each of these is a Pomodoro. After four Pomodoros, you can have a longer break of 20 minutes (Hagan, 2016).

Eight Ways to Develop Extreme Self-Discipline

Discipline is key to self and group leadership. Focus and self-discipline bring happiness, achievement, and contentment. Below are eight essential steps to develop self-discipline for a growth mind-set.

Recognize Your Strengths and Weaknesses

Everyone has flaws. Whether it's alcohol, tobacco, junk food, social media, or Netflix, all affect us similarly. Weaknesses aren't merely lack of self-control. . Each of us has areas where we excel as well as areas where we kind of fail.

Self-awareness expands your comfort zone, but it needs ongoing focus and accepting your weaknesses. Too frequently, people pretend their vulnerabilities don't exist or submit to them with a fixed mindset, saying, "Oh well." Know your strengths, but more significantly, accept your flaws. You must conquer them.

Eliminate Temptations

Removing your main temptations will increase your self-discipline. Throw away junk food to eat healthier. Want to consume less alcohol? Get rid of the alcohol. Turn off social media notifications, silent your phone, and organize your to-do list better if you want to increase your productivity at work. Set goals and carry them out. You will be more focused on achieving your goals if there are less distractions around. Get rid of negative influences to position yourself for success.

Plan and Set Goals

Self-discipline requires a clear vision, just like any goal. Define success for yourself. After all, it's simple to become lost or diverted if you don't know where you're heading. Consider your priorities.

A plan specifies time-bound steps to attain your goals. This strategy helps successful people stay on track, connect emotionally to their objective, and set a clear finish line.

Be Consistent

Self-discipline is learnt, not something you are born with. It demands regular practice and repetition, like any other talent. It should be routine. Self-discipline calls for effort and concentration, which can be exhausting. It can get harder and harder to maintain your willpower as time goes on. It can feel harder to do other duties that call for restraint the stronger the temptation or decision is.

Develop self-discipline by working daily toward a goal. Plan your everyday diligence. Whatever works for you, put it on your calendar, to-do list, or on your refrigerator.

Develop New Routines and Habits

Developing self-discipline and forming a new habit can be difficult if you focus on the entire endeavor. Keep things basic so that you won't feel intimidated. Make your objective into manageable, little steps. Focus on performing one thing consistently and develop self-discipline with that objective in mind rather than trying to alter everything at once.

If you don't exercise often, start with 10 to 15 minutes a day. Start going to bed 30 minutes earlier to improve your sleep pattern. Change your shopping habits and meal prep to eat healthier. Then, when your perspective and habits change, add more goals.

Change How You Think About Willpower

If you have limited willpower, you won't push yourself. Studies reveal that willpower can decrease with time (Clemson, 2020). But what about modifying our perception of willpower?

When we adopt the concept of unrestricted willpower, we continue to develop, accomplish more, and strengthen our mental toughness. In other words, our internal ideas about self-control and willpower can influence how disciplined we are. You'll offer yourself a greater incentive to achieve those goals if you can get rid of these established barriers and have faith in your ability to succeed.

Plan Beforehand

Psychologists use a method called "implementation intention" to enhance willpower. It involves planning how to handle a potentially tough scenario.

Say you want to be a hair stylist but tell yourself, "I probably won't excel, so I'll stick with tailoring." That's a poor backup plan wrapped in mediocrity. Keep pushing forward with confidence. Plan ahead to gain the right mindset and self-discipline. You'll save energy by avoiding emotive decisions.

Forgive Yourself and Move On

We sometimes fail despite our best intentions and efforts. You'll have triumphs and missteps. However, keep going. If you stumble, ask the five WHYs to identify the underlying cause before continuing. Avoid getting bogged down in feelings of regret, resentment, or fury since they will only make you feel worse and prevent you from moving forward.

Recognize your mistakes and forgive yourself. Then return to the game and carry out your execution with ferocity. This will lead you to success!

Additional Tips For Self-Discipline

Finally, in your quest to develop greater self-discipline, you might want some additional tips on how you can improve. You can try some of the following suggestions:

- **Keep going**: Success never comes easily or in a straight line. It's crucial to develop the ability to endure discomfort and learn from your errors. Just because you made a mistake doesn't indicate you're a failure or that you can't succeed; it merely reveals a potential area for improvement. Adjust your strategy as necessary, decide what has to be improved, and move forward.

- **Use positive talk**: Positive affirmations can keep you upbeat and help you remember why it's crucial to carry out your plans. Examples of affirmations are "I will do what needs to be done, even when I don't feel like it," and "I have the discipline to attain my goals."

- **Reward yourself**: Just like with goal setting, when you achieve success, it's crucial to treat yourself. Celebrating your successes will keep things enjoyable and boost your urge to press on.

- **Be confident**: Don't let occasional setbacks or a fear of failing demotivate you. Failure and setbacks are a part of life for all of us. Recognize your mistake, take a lesson from it, and move on.

Lost My Oomph

Say, for example, a goal you set didn't go the way you planned. Which would you pick—motivation or discipline—if you could only choose one? Which would put you back on track?

Most times, you'll be let down by motivation. Yes, although motivation is the driving force that excites you, what happens when the excitement is gone by two or three mistakes?

Not that motivation is not significantly important, but you'll always have self-discipline on your side. Your ability to successfully navigate the treacherous battlefield of life is only made possible by developing self-discipline.

Your Mind Is Always Directing You in The Right Direction

You have some sort of objective in mind at all times when you are awake. The prefrontal cortex, which is located in the front of the brain, serves as the CEO. Your conduct is programmed to help you achieve that goal.

As we know, your long-term goals help you develop as a person and move you toward success while your short-term goals help you get through your daily life.

The CEO of your brain must use self-discipline mechanisms to combat distractions as you maintain focus on your objective. And, to no surprise at all, one of the distractions it might face is fading motivation.

Being Motivated Isn't Always Simple

Your motivation will decrease and you'll give up if the pleasure of something in your environment tempts you more than the joy of achieving your goal, or if momentary difficulty along the way eclipses the reward of the goal at the finish.

You cannot be a motivational puppet in the battlefield or in daily life. You need to have the ability to overcome low motivation if it interferes with your purpose. Too much hunger can occasionally make you unmotivated. Sometimes you lose motivation if you're too exhausted. However, you put your life in peril if you let your waning motivation dictate your actions.

When There Is No Longer Any Motivation, How Do You Continue?

Self-discipline is the only factor that can overcome a lack of motivation. It pertains to discipline, remaining steadfast, knowing what needs to be done, and bringing it about.

The prefrontal cortex, your brain's CEO, performs this function. Unaffected by distractions, it stays on course, knows what needs to be done, and takes action to do it.

Self-discipline will always get you where you want to go.

Chapter 4:

The Winning Formula

Acknowledging that we all have strengths and weaknesses and knowing how to use these to our advantage can improve our chances of success. This is due to the fact that they are important predictors of our attitudes, mindset, and behavior.

The world we live in now is ever changing. The world's options and knowledge are constantly growing as a result of social media, simple communication methods, and globalization.

Making the best decision can be incredibly challenging and complex without having a good understanding of your own preferences. Everyone has a different personality, and understanding what makes us who we are can help us make better decisions in life and achieve more success on both a personal and professional level.

In this chapter, we will look at strengths and weaknesses, and how these can help us in achieving our growth mindset.

On The Offense

Every person is unique, and our personalities have an impact on how we behave. Finding your strengths and getting to know yourself are vital. You may capitalize on your strengths and use them to advance in both your personal and professional lives. However, this does not imply that these weaknesses will be your undoing. There is need for improvement in these areas. It is not something you lack; rather, it is something you must grow and develop. Finding your strengths is the first step in using your strengths and enhancing your weaknesses.

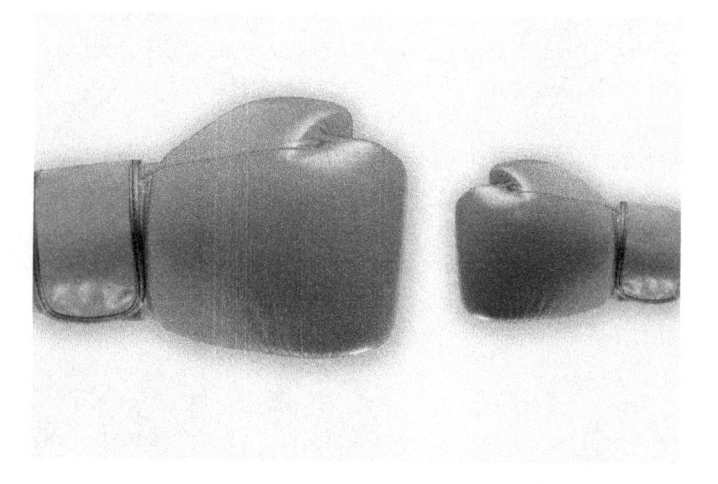

One of your greatest personal strengths would be something you do extremely naturally. Think about what comes naturally to you for a while; it may be anything. You might have little trouble striking up conversation with strangers or be very skilled at finding solutions in a sticky situation. Despite what your strengths are, they all play a role in how we think, perceive situations and carry out daily life.

The Importance Of Strengths

As we might've guessed, strengths are essential to productivity and success. But what exactly makes them special and distinct from our actual personalities? Here is a list of the importance of strengths.

Time-Saving

Being aware of the strengths and skills you possess will enable you to make immediate decision-making and saves you the time and hassle of going back and forth with a decision or situation.

Increases Growth

Knowing your strengths and areas of proficiency can enable you to expand your horizons and achieve new heights. If you merely understand your strengths, you can accomplish much more than you ever imagined.

Boosts Confidence

Whatever they may be, identifying your strong areas will help you feel more confident. Even if they are minor talents, they will boost your confidence, which will enable you to accomplish more.

Enhances Happiness

Knowing your strengths makes you feel confident and capable. Anyone will be pleased knowing they have a skill set that will provide them an advantage.

You Can Inspire Others

When you know your own strengths, you can inspire or assist others. Setting an example or being an inspiration to others is an essential self-actualization prospect of life, so it will not only benefit the person, but you as well.

How to Identify and Use Your Strengths

Asking yourself and those around you some questions about who you are, your talents, and your hobbies is one of the greatest ways to help you identify what kinds of strengths you possess. But there are other ways to recognize and use your strengths. Here are five pointers to get you going:

Investigate

Ask individuals you trust, and respect what you're best at to learn more about yourself. They could be family members, teachers, or friends. Make a list of the most prevalent qualities they stated, and investigate why. When you are aware of your strengths, make an effort to uphold or continue this trait, and if possible, improve it.

Discover Your Personality

Take a personality test, write a journal or play around with quizzes and games to see what best suits you. Of course, we all know who we are, but discovering our personality type and highlighting some of our qualities can help us to know and use our strengths. For example, knowing if you are introverted or extroverted may make some strengths and weaknesses significantly clearer.

Take Notes

Write down your five favorite things to do during the week. Why do you enjoy them? For instance: "I keep a blog that I update frequently with thoughts, stories, news, and other information I find online. I organize writing and content-finding time each week, after which I schedule social media postings with links to my website."

It's obvious that this person enjoys organization, keeps up with pop culture, and works well alone in this situation. Considering the activities you enjoy can help you determine your strengths and skills.

Note Patterns

From using the techniques mentioned above, identify common areas or character qualities. Your strongest strengths are probably your most-used ones.

Be Flexible

Some answers and findings may be shocking or reveal unconsidered areas of your personality, including weaknesses. Don't disregard it. The goal is to better understand yourself, including your public image, your strengths, and your weaknesses. These unexpected qualities may be useful in other situations.

On The Defense

We all have weaknesses despite our wishes. Everyone has elements of their lives that need more attention. However, with time and work, they can become strengths. If you focus on your weaknesses, you can hurt your self-confidence. Accept their existence, then decide what to do.

Why Weaknesses Matter and How to Identify Them

You can better understand yourself and how you work if you are aware of your own strengths and weaknesses.

However, knowing your weaknesses helps you identify potential barriers to advancement, which allows you to discover solutions to avoid falling behind due to them.

A weakness doesn't mean you have no strengths. Simply put, it signifies you typically possess less of that strength. Alternatively, it could imply that one component of you isn't as strong as your other assets.

Find Your Weakness

If a strength is not developed, it corresponds to a weakness. Make a list of your flaws (or underdeveloped strengths) that could help you accomplish your goals next. For instance, you might not be a good cook. You don't need to include it as a weakness if it has nothing to do with your objectives.

Start by compiling a list of the following to better understand your weaknesses:

- **Insufficient skills:** These could be learned through training and experience.

- **Soft skills**: You may see how acquiring these talents could help you attain your goals or enhance your health.

- **Flaws**: These are your specific struggles.

- **Identifying vulnerabilities**: Notice what you're avoiding. What do you do? What do you avoid? If you regularly put off the same crucial duties without a valid explanation, it may mean you haven't mastered them.

Review Feedback For Patterns

Consider past performance reviews and manager and coworker feedback. Do patterns emerge? If multiple people have told you the same thing, you may need to improve on that area.

It's important to have professional and personal relationships with people who will tell you the truth. They don't have to be your best friends, but they must be honest, trustworthy, and willing to criticize you.

Get to The Punch Line

If you're often the target of jokes about your disorganization or tardiness, it may be because others are trying to rectify these faults through humor. Listen to individuals around you for signs about what bothers them, then examine if they could hold you back.

Find Past failures

Success isn't all sunny leaps forward. The best performers overcame slight failures to advance. You can't improve until you analyze your prior failure, and it might not be pleasant. But if you can see the situation for what it is—warts and all—you can see what part you played. This reveals problem regions. Then, reframe them as skills you want to develop.

Turning Weaknesses Into Strengths

Having weaknesses only means we're human. But we don't have to live with them and walk on ice whenever we remember they exist. We can take these weaknesses and transform them into strengths.

Perhaps they won't work for every single weakness in our lives, because then we'd be 'perfect.' But turning certain weaknesses into strengths in order to increase productivity and success is a keen start. Consider this a tool for the future.

Step One: Deep Dive

After identifying your primary flaws, investigate further. You want to know *why* that area is weak. What makes the activity or feature of yourself a weakness? For example, you may wish to overcome procrastination. You've already identified the issue, but why does it happen? Is it anxiety about the task? Perhaps you're not motivated to do it. Sit down with your flaws and determine what makes them, then, you can understand how to change them.

Step Two: Make a Plan

Looking back won't assist you any longer. It's time to look ahead and ask, "How can I turn my weakness into a strength?"

There are a ton of different approaches you might take, as well as several tools and methods. However, regardless of the challenge you are facing or the resources you employ, one reality always holds true:

You must make a consistent, conscious effort!

Without effort, nothing will change. The weakness isn't a strength for a reason. You haven't mastered it.

Focused practice is needed to make it a strength. Hence, create a realistic action plan.

However, don't overextend yourself. Make sure you can follow the strategy you develop. It serves little use to work on a skill for three days at an eight-hour a day pace only to give up from exhaustion. Over the course of weeks and months, fifteen minutes a day will provide amazing benefits! Draw up a plan of action to transform your shortcomings into strengths, then go to work.

Step Three: Attack Limiting Beliefs

You might be working hard to turn your flaws into strengths with your new plan. But there's another thing to consider. There are beliefs you currently have about yourself. Over the years, these have cemented themselves in your memory. Because our brains enjoy harmony, it will eventually find its way back to that state. This implies that our behavior should reflect our values.

We must change our self-perception by attacking our limiting beliefs. Self-talk and mental images are helpful. Self-talk changes how you talk to yourself. Your mental conversation changes as a result, greatly changing how you view yourself.

Mental imagery is the next step. Now, imagery is effective because it mimics how our brains react to a real-life situation. As a result, you can educate your mind to imagine you doing differently so that it will believe it truly happened.

You'll be astounded by the difference in your mindset after practicing both of them over time. Over time, doing both will change your mind.

Be On Guard

Although strengths and weaknesses can be beneficial to you once you have learned how to utilize them, this might also be a breeding ground for manipulation from others. People around you might seek to use your strengths or even more your weaknesses to use against you. So, it is important that we stay on guard.

How to Recognize The Intention of Others

There are two ways you can identify someone's true intentions, whether they are good or bad:

- Analyze the person's behavior toward you and other individuals to try to determine what they are doing. You can then observe how you or the individuals or group they are interacting with respond. This response or reaction from you or the other people is what they are getting out of their actions.

- Consider and determine the outcomes that a person's behavior is bringing about if their activities are now concealed or unknown.

In short, the two ways to determine someone's intentions are through:

- Their behavior.
- Or the effects of their actions.

To determine the impartial truth, it is preferable if you can accomplish both.

How to Protect Yourself From Those Who Want to Manipulate You

Even when we try to identify and avoid them, it still might be hard to protect ourselves from those with ill intentions, since they aren't good for our productivity and life overall. Here are a few additional tips to help you avoid such individuals.

Remember Your Goals and Priorities

Manipulators are self-serving; thus they'll try to change or dismiss your dream. This includes telling you you won't succeed or pressing you to tackle projects below your ability or outside your chosen route.

Daily clarify your goals and the objective of each task so the manipulator can't sway you. This focus will keep you from being emotionally attached if the manipulator causes logistical or relationship problems.

Communicate Your Intention

In relation to the aforementioned point, manipulators could try to spread false information about you or your job or they might withhold information that you require to proceed appropriately. But the more you verbally or in writing share your goals and beliefs, the harder it is for a manipulator to turn others against you.

You define yourself, not the manipulator. The more witnesses you have, the better. Always back up and preserve your records.

Call It As You See It

Even if they're terrified of failing, manipulators do badly because they assume they won't get caught. They cling to their egos and convince themselves they're too skillful with systems and people to get caught, or they believe that because they've never faced a consequence, they can continue to evade it. Tell them what you've seen and how it's affected you to shatter their delusion.

To prepare for your encounter, track the manipulator's offenses, including dates, actions, and names. The encounter needn't be harsh. Simply give the options for moving forward after thoughtfully outlining the facts. Once the manipulator is conscious that you are aware, they will be less inclined to try to manipulate you in the future, especially if you mention the possibility of making the proper reports to superiors or HR.

In the end, you will need a strong mindset to be on your guard, develop strengths, and change weaknesses. And in turn, you'll find yourself in an advantageous loop, when this helps you to grow your mindset as well.

Chapter 5:

Life is Unpredictable

At any point, our plans can be interrupted and we have to be able to respond quickly or adapt in order to avoid being thrown completely off course. Life is an unpredictable train, heading towards an ultimate destination, but might take different, unexpected roads to get there.

Our job is not to wallow and cry about the unexpected occurrences, and even sometimes, failures, but to use our mindsets and find a way around it, through it, under it or over it. We have to know how to adapt to changes, and stay resilient and focused. In this chapter, I will show you how.

The Going Gets Tough

Life has different stages. You will have periods of pure contentment and a sense of direction in your life. You will know that you're surrounded by the right kind of people and the best circumstances to do this, and you will have a plan for accomplishing your goals and aspirations.

But sometimes you could feel trapped. You might have a sneaking suspicion that something is odd, or you might even be aware of which aspects of your life are out of control.

The first thing to do if you are experiencing these feelings is to determine precisely what is wrong and the reason you're feeling this way. This will then provide you the opportunity to act to remedy the situation. It's also important to understand that these things happen everyday, to almost everyone. Even in the simplest things, such as planning to have cereal for breakfast, but discovering that you have no milk.

The point is, everyone has their fair share of challenges in life, and it all boils down to who they are, how you live, and what you do about it. No two challenges are the same, so understanding that life happens unexpectedly sometimes is the first step in overcoming the feeling of dread when something doesn't go the way you want it to.

But can you detect or control it before it completely crumbles? How can you be certain that something is amiss before it blows up, and what exactly do you do about it?

Here are seven warning signs that your life might be going off track, and what you can do to overcome it.

You Complain Nonstop

Negativity is a warning sign that something is wrong. It frequently serves as a red flag for mental problems including anxiety, stress, or depression. The worst aspect about negativity is that it can really change how the brain functions, making a person more vulnerable to depression.

How to Respond to This:

Try to identify the source of your bad feelings and then take action to get rid of it. In some circumstances, changing your lifestyle, removing a toxic individual from your daily life, or quitting a bad habit will cause you to change right away.

Life might be challenging at times, making it difficult to pinpoint or eliminate the cause of your negativity. If so, make an effort to emphasize the things that make you happy and joyful. Maybe you could spend some time with uplifting friends or take a break to unwind. You'll feel more empowered if you take charge of the areas of your life that you can change.

Your Loved Ones Don't Make You Happy

Your interactions with friends and family should bring you delight. It won't always be about having fun and laughing, just like in any relationship. We all have to learn to accept the good with the bad, and sometimes others around us will need your help. Your close interactions should, overall, still be fulfilling.

How to Respond to This:

Ask yourself why you don't feel fulfilled by your friendships if you don't. Perhaps you need to expand your network of friends. Alternatively, maybe you have too many superficial connections and should put more effort into your few meaningful relationships with your closest friends and family.

You will come across poisonous people from time to time. Perhaps they encourage you to partake in harmful or even risky behaviors. They could lower your self-esteem with their words or actions toward you.

Find out who these people are, and then figure out how to either lessen their influence on you or get rid of them entirely. You'll have more time and energy as a result to devote to relationships that boost your self-esteem and advance your development.

You Hate Going to Work

It may be time to reconsider your arrangements if you are constantly unhappy at work. Even while it's common to feel a little blue once the weekend is over, it might be worthwhile to investigate the causes if you have anxiety when traveling to work or feel sick at the mere notion of your job or position.

How to Respond to This:

In a perfect world, everyone could profit handsomely from what they love to do. This isn't always feasible, though. If your job is truly making you unhappy, there is probably a better option for you if you make the commitment to look for it.

Even the simple act of seeking for a better option will probably give you a sense of empowerment and put you back in charge of your destiny.

You Put Unachieved Goals On Hold

Having a purpose helps us stay focused and gets us out of bed with a good attitude. A sense of purpose can also operate as a "protective factor" when things go wrong. Our sense of purpose can help us put setbacks, disappointments, and difficulties into perspective so that we can keep moving forward.

It can be alluring to postpone your goals and aspirations while you wait for the ideal situation to present itself. In actuality, you might waste time waiting for something that may never happen.

How to Respond to This:

Take your aspirations and goals seriously. Commit to making a change for the better right now to assist you achieve those objectives. Instead than getting overly focused on not having arrived at the destination, celebrate each small victory along the journey. The trip might be really enjoyable.

You're Not Making The Most of Your Free Time

We all have various amounts of free time, but it's crucial that we use it to do things we like or that improve our wellbeing when we do have it.

According to studies, those who participate in leisure activities have lower stress levels, better moods, lower heart rates, and more psychological engagement—that is, less boredom, which can assist in avoiding hazardous behaviors (Guest, 2021).

It is common to have a few obligations and duties that you must complete on your own time. However, if at all possible, spend a significant percentage of your free time engaging in activities you enjoy. It is worthwhile to reevaluate your work-life balance if this is not attainable. Your total productivity is likely to increase if you can find the time to put your mental and physical health first.

How to Respond to This:

Record your leisure activities and evaluate them to determine if you can make any improvements. Are you wasting time on activities that don't provide much value? Could you change your priorities to make more time for the activities you enjoy the most? What could you change so that you could enjoy and feel fulfilled during the day even more?

You should make an effort to spend at least some of your free time doing something you truly enjoy. You'll benefit emotionally from having a mental break from the stresses of daily life as a result.

You're Not Acting in a Way That Honors Your Principles

We all have various sets of values.

Some people will prioritize supporting their families above all else. Others will find fulfillment in their work or a cause close to their hearts. The likelihood of feeling resentful or unfulfilled is much decreased when you are doing things you love and that are important to you.

On the other side, you are likely to feel some level of discomfort or unhappiness if your way of life, attitude, or behavior indicates that you aren't living your life in accordance with your fundamental beliefs and values. Your emotional health will start to suffer once you realize that you aren't being genuine to yourself. Therefore, if you value honesty yet are being dishonest with those around you, your conscience is going to be very troubled by this.

How to Respond to This:

To conduct your own "values audit," follow the guidelines below:

- List your top five values.

- List the ways in which you behave in accordance with your values.

- Make a second list of the actions you are taking that go against these principles.

Determine what needs to be improved by comparing these three lists. Consider ways to extend the amount of time you spend acting in accordance with your values and ways to stop doing things that don't.

Use this as the foundation for a brief action plan that details how you can live more in line with your values. It doesn't matter how it looks.

You're Doubting Yourself

The moment of truth has arrived.

It's likely that you know deep down that something isn't quite right if you've felt like your life is going off track, or unpredictable things happen and you have no idea how to approach it.

It is entirely normal to experience times in your life when you are not entirely content. To aim for perpetual happiness and nonstop fulfillment is unrealistic. However, if a particular aspect of your life consistently makes you unhappy, you have the ability to make changes for the better. The best person to figure things out and make the necessary changes to get your life back on track is you.

How to Respond to This:

When you experience this, keep in mind that while you may not always have control over your circumstances, you always have control over how you choose to react to them.

Everything can be taken from a man except one thing: to choose one's own way. We have the ability to select our reactions to life's changes.

Be careful to acknowledge your progress along the road and feel proud of the steps you are taking to better your life.

Not everyone who is successful is the happiest person. They are the ones who maximize their resources and adapt accordingly to life's changes.

The Tough Get Going

Everything we achieve is based on a growth mindset. A person's mindset (not their skill set) is what they believe to be true on a regular basis. On the other hand, conservative viewpoints, pessimism, the avoidance of risk, and anxiety-related mindsets correspond with those who find excuses and give in.

According to research, learning how to bounce, grow, connect, and find flow is a set of interconnected skills (Hartnell-Young, 2020). A growth minded individual tackles tasks that get harder and harder. Failure and adversity are inevitable. So instead of using this as an excuse to give in, we need to develop forward action to combat these setbacks.

The New Zealand All Blacks rugby team practices these techniques with the motto "red or blue, decide, do." This is the discipline of approaching a difficult situation knowing that they have a 'red' emotional reactionary approach or a 'blue' calm and deliberate approach to select from. This allows players to acquire a better perspective, and play with full commitment and careful thought (Hartnell-Young, 2020).

A Willingness to Consider All Options

A growth mindset's resilience component is established on the understanding that challenges will always exist. Events and environment changes can erect significant obstacles. Resilience entails changing the course, keeping an eye out for opportunities to the left and right, and leaving room for them.

No matter your fame, wealth, or skills, you will face challenges in life. However, you get to decide how you will respond to those challenges. Personal development and mental tranquility result from learning how to deal with problems in healthy, beneficial ways. In order to deal with life's obstacles, consider these four healthy strategies:

- Stop overthinking.
- Utilizing your strengths.
- Accepting change.

Stop Overthinking

It is normal to do some deep self-searching when difficulties come up in our life in an effort to find solutions to lessen the discomfort and misery the problems cause. However, the longer you think about a scenario or problem, the more unhappy and agitated you will feel, and the more probable it is that you won't have found a solution. Additionally, it has been shown that overthinking hinders problem-solving, depletes motivation, and worsens or prolongs depressive symptoms (Schramm, n.d).

Overthinking should be avoided at all costs. Here are nine methods you can use the next time you want to break out of an overthinking cycle:

- **Get distracted**: Find a pleasant (and safe) activity to engage in when you become aware that you are overthinking to entirely distract your focus. You may watch a movie, clean the kitchen, go for a run, or simply hang out with your coworkers. Sometimes all that is required is getting up and moving to a different room.

- **Change the way you think**: When you catch yourself overthinking, tell yourself 'STOP!' in your head, out loud, or both. Find something else to focus about after that that won't stress you out.

- **Set a timer**: Every day, allot 15–30 minutes to thinking too much. You'll be less likely to overthink the rest of the day if you know that there will be a set period of time for it. The optimum time to set aside for overthinking is definitely not right before bed or when you are feeling anxious or depressed.

- **Chat with a friend**: Find a compassionate and reliable person with whom you can discuss your concerns. Sometimes all it takes to clear your mind is to just express your thoughts. Be prepared to listen to your friend's views and problems without passing judgment.

- **Write it down**: Write down your ideas so you can arrange and interpret them. Overthinking makes thinking more difficult, but writing your thoughts down helps the dust to settle so you can identify the true issues.

- **Replace your worrying thoughts**: Learning to replace persistently negative ideas with either neutral or positive ones is the key to achieving true mental peace. Keep in mind that difficult experiences in your life do not define who you are. Do not look for the cracks, especially when you are depressed. Your mental resources are depleted when you overthink, making it challenging to focus on other tasks.

- **Fix what can be fixed**: Make an effort to address the issues that were generating your overthinking, even if it's just a small step. If necessary, you might make a list of all potential fixes for the issue. Instead of waiting for things to happen, take action. You will feel better as a result.

- **Determine your triggers**: Find out what people or circumstances make you overthink, and avoid them or change the situation so that it no longer makes you overthink.

- **Consider the bigger picture**: Asking yourself whether what you are thinking about will matter in a year will help you have a larger perspective of the situation. If what you are obsessing over is important, consider what you can learn from this experience.

Utilize Your Strengths

From the previous chapter, you probably would have acknowledged your limitations and weaknesses. However, concentrating on these flaws does not provide fruitful results. Instead, concentrate on your own, personal skills. Finding these strengths and knowing how to apply them in the right circumstances can improve your self-esteem and outlook on life.

Take into account the following actions to maximize your strengths:

- **Determine your strong points**: Make a list of your strengths after giving it some thought. You might accomplish this on your own by asking a close friend or member of your family to assist you in identifying them. Whatever strategy you choose, make a list of your top strengths because acknowledging them is the first step to being able to utilize them.

- **Reflect**: Consider how you could use your strengths to get over life's obstacles. Also think about how you may utilize your strengths in new and distinctive ways.

- **Establish objectives**: Make a strategy to use one of your strengths as frequently as you can. You might spend the entire week concentrating on one strength, or you could focus on a new strength each day.

- **Analyze**: After carrying out your plan, reflect on your experience while concentrating on your strengths. Write about your event, highlighting both your feelings and the lessons you took away. More goals should be set in order to keep playing to your strengths. Find a way to modify something that didn't work out so well so that it now serves a useful purpose.

Accept Change

Change will always occur. Your job will give you new duties, your marriage might experience difficulties, and your roles in life will change. Even good things like a promotion, a birth or adoption, or a new home can lead to internal conflict. It might be difficult to adjust to a new normal due to changes in personal circumstances or the political environment. You could experience a range of emotions, from happiness to melancholy and depression.

Using these five suggestions to get through turbulent times is a superior strategy:

- **Think ahead**: If you are aware that change is coming, get ready. When you have a backup plan in place, change is less stressful.

- **Stop and think**: Most individuals don't take the time to recognize what they're losing before jumping onto something new because of today's hectic schedules. Give your ideas a voice instead of masking your unhappiness with new distractions.

- **Try to keep things somewhat normal**: The more you can stick to your tried-and-true schedule during a life change, the more comfortable structure and routine will be for you.

- **Create comfort**: Include fun and stress-reducing activities in your day. Take a warm bath, go to the gym, meditate, or listen to soothing music. Whatever you choose as long as it's reassuring to you and healthy is all that matters. Avoid using unhealthy practices like smoking, drinking, or gambling to numb uncomfortable emotions.

- **Count blessings**: Writing down your blessings in a gratitude diary will significantly reduce your sense of exhaustion. Things like appreciating a starry sky, a peaceful sunset, or a pretty butterfly can serve almost like a reset button for your mind even during difficult circumstances.

Be patient with yourself; breaking the habit of overthinking will take time and effort. You will gradually start to notice improvement in your own wellbeing as well as in your interactions with others as you put in persistent effort to combat your overthinking.

Additionally, even though it's crucial to work on your weaknesses, concentrating on playing to your strengths will boost your confidence. You will grow stronger and more prepared to handle life's obstacles as you put more of your attention on playing to your strengths.

And finally, learn to accept change, and when or if life takes an unexpected turn, you will be capable and prepared in accepting and navigating this change. Things happen out of place all the time, and our plans may not always go how we wish them to. But, in the end, the only option we truly have is accepting it, and finding a way to make it work for us.

Chapter 6:

The Sky Is Not The Limit

People with growth mindsets are always looking for ways to push their limits and improve their performance. We tend to use the word 'potential' frequently in a variety of contexts, but what does it actually mean when applied to people? Is it crucial for us to realize our own personal potential, whatever it may be?

Potential refers to the possibility and capacity for something to occur. But is the idea applicable when considering someone's life in this way? I believe this is the case because, if someone has the capacity to achieve greatness in life, shouldn't they exert every effort to accomplish so? In a perfect world, they would do everything in their power to make this happen. But regrettably, things are rarely so straightforward because other factors might also be at play. This, however, doesn't mean we should settle. Settling is more of a fixed mindset than growth.

So, how can we do this?

In this chapter, we will look at how we can reach our full potential while using a growth mindset. We don't have to settle for the metamorphic 'sky.' There is a vast universe out there just waiting to be discovered.

Turn Up The Notch

It is up to each individual to live their lives, whether they make the most of any information or talents they may possess or not. Because what if someone believes they can't fulfill their potential but still wants to? There may be a variety of causes for this, but self-doubt could be a significant one. Self-doubt, a lack of self-confidence, and many other self-generated obstacles can prevent someone from realizing their full potential in any skill they may have.

But it's time to shake off self-doubt, and strive toward growing more and more as an individual. True, it is easier said than done, but if you have a growth mindset, you are halfway there.

How to Reach Your Full Potential

The belief that there is no more opportunity for development or improvement is a significant barrier to the success that so many people want in life and business.

Here are three ideas to assist you in reaching your full potential:

Change The Way You Think

This is first because, if you don't change your thinking, nothing else will ever change. The first thing that needs attention if you're unhappy with where you are in life right now is the caliber of your ideas.

People who don't reach their full potential throughout their time on earth typically have severe cognitive deficiencies. They utterly disregard the value of mentality growth and the necessity of treating the mind like a gold mine, in addition to lacking the kind of thinking necessary to achieve all that is possible in life.

Each of us possesses brilliance, but whether that genius is developed depends on what happens every day from the neck up. Never limiting what's possible is the first step to creating a bigger future and realizing your potential. More than anything else, a person's mindset and way of thinking can obstruct greatness. Change your thoughts before you can change your life.

Be Obsessive About Learning New Things All The Time

Do not behave in a common manner. The majority of people stop studying as soon as they complete their official schooling. They lack a personal growth plan that details how and when they will advance each month. Sadly, most people become entrenched in their old habits and will continue to produce the same outcomes until their time is up.

Invest in becoming a lifelong learner if you're serious about realizing your potential and becoming everything you can be.

Enroll in online classes, read excellent books in your profession, listen to audiobooks while driving, and continually look for opportunities to grow personally. One of the best decisions you can ever make is choosing to pursue learning as a lifelong endeavor. A significant barrier that will keep you stuck in the current place you are functioning out of is the belief that you are an expert in everything or that there is no potential for improvement.

People who sincerely feel they have attained their full potential in life and as individuals never make the effort to reinvest in themselves and pursue lifelong learning. Make sure that's not you.

Create a Winning Team to Support You

People are important, and great organizations and their leaders are aware of this. A successful CEO is aware that for his or her business to succeed, the people working there must also be striving, developing, and seeking for ways to excel.

Your life is affected in the same way. The people around us determine how wonderful we can become as individuals. Associating and surrounding yourself with successful people, those who are succeeding at a level that you aspire to, is a certain approach to realize your full potential.

Make a list of people who make up your personal team. Write down whether each person is actually assisting you in developing and reaching your goals next to their names.

Many people, including myself, get so wrapped up in our busy lives that we rarely take the time to consider our social circles. You'll be able to identify one or two folks who no longer serve your best interests. If you want to maximize your potential and develop into an exceptional achiever, you must first assemble a winning team around you.

Our potential and levels of performance stagnate when we stop looking for new opportunities to improve.

What Is Brain Plasticity and Why Is It So Crucial?

Having a "growth mindset" is believing that you can improve and change at any time. The term 'neuroplasticity' or brain plasticity describes your brain's capacity to develop and alter over time as a result of exposure to new information. Saying that a growth mindset pushes you to attempt new things will help you make the connection between the ideas. Your brain's neuroplasticity can be aided by engaging in activities that are associated with a growth mindset.

How Does Neuroplasticity Function and What Is It?

People believed that the brain stopped developing at a particular age for a very long period. However, the brain can now grow and change at any age. These changes happen gradually.

When you first try anything new, your brain may undergo certain chemical changes.

The longer you study and develop new skills, the more likely it is that your brain will continue to undergo physical changes. Your brain's structure can alter over time as a result of new connections formed by neurons.

The longer you practice these habits, the stronger and more active your brain grows. Remember that the brain can undergo both positive and negative changes. If the brain is not stimulated, its capabilities may decline.

How Can Neuroplasticity Help Develop a Growth Mindset?

A growth mindset is something you can acquire at any time in your life. For a growth mindset, absorbing new information, and acquiring new skills can frequently boost neuroplasticity.

Trying new things and broadening your horizons might encourage mental and cognitive development. These kinds of activities could be:

- Taking up a new hobby.
- Studying a second language.
- Reading a book on a new subject.
- Traveling to new places.
- Going to an art gallery.

Be aware that changes in the brain and perspective take time to manifest. You cannot participate in one of the aforementioned activities for a little amount of time and expect to see any kind of significant change. The development of neuronal circuits is aided by practice and repetition.

To reap the rewards of both, resolve to constantly try new things and be open to new experiences. Keep in mind that doing anything new is not about becoming the best at it. Instead, it's about pushing yourself to continue learning throughout your life. Your brain and general health can both benefit greatly from this.

You're My Inspiration

The world is full of opportunities, and success, and sometimes it happens to those around us more than ourselves. We've probably all done this a number of times: checking our friend's Facebook updates of their fantastic new jobs or admission to prestigious institutions. We probably also see someone's marriage, new vehicle, adorable child, and the list continues.

You'll start to think about your own life and what you've done with it—or rather, what you haven't done—when you see your peers start to take similar actions.

Like we discussed in the previous chapter, you'll probably feel left behind and thinking that you are regressing in comparison to others. You might even be jealous and resentful of others' success, prestige, and possession.

But there are many reasons why success should be praised rather than denigrated. Here are three comprehensive reasons why we should react positively to other people's successes.

Learn From Others

Work to attract respect and goodwill, as encouragement is essential. Ask others who are already doing what you wish to accomplish for guidance and suggestions. For example, if you want to propose to your girlfriend, you can ask your friend who has recently tied the knot for suggestions on acquiring a wedding ring, a great place to set the mood and how to secure a happy, and with as little stress as possible engagement period.

Get as much free advice as you can; the folks you ask will probably be delighted to assist. These people are aware of the benefits of cooperation, teamwork, and idea exchange. Make sure you don't repeat their errors by utilizing their knowledge.

Absorb Success

We all hope that success could spread like the common cold. Unfortunately, this is not how life operates; nonetheless, spending time with contented and prosperous individuals might motivate you to fulfill your potential.

Naturally, chance and luck play a part in our lives, but it's also important to take advantage of opportunities, use your resources wisely, adapt, and make the best of any circumstances you may encounter.

Take action and observe the outcomes.

You truly are a byproduct of the people you associate with. Although we could have grandiose fantasies, if your pals aren't pushing themselves and live up to their potential, chances are that you also aren't.

Spending time with and learning from ambitious, driven, and successful individuals will help you start to adapt and eventually embrace their way of thinking. Put yourself in circumstances that have the potential to be exciting and profitable.

By doing this, you'll be able to sort of absorb the successful characteristics of others around you and apply them to your own way of life.

Envy Is Ineffective

Envy of others won't change how successful they are; it will just make you feel discouraged and prolong your own lack of achievement. Instead of generating and taking opportunities, you are squandering time.

You will never be able to know the full tale, so avoid comparing your life to anyone else's. This will simply cause you to question every choice you make, which will further stall your progress toward achievement and development.

Keep the negativity at a distance because it will only serve to lower your spirits. Look at other people's accomplishments with optimism, not envy. Let their achievements inspire you to persevere and be determined. Your life will be better if you are loyal to yourself.

Consistent Rebirth

In order to achieve our goals, consistency is not always simple to maintain. But in order to achieve these objectives, consistency is frequently the one factor that matters the most.

It forces you to remain in the present, encourages you to concentrate on your controllable actions, and serves as a reminder that growth and expansion occur throughout the process, not as a result.

You don't suddenly transform into a comedian the moment you take the stage; rather, you develop into one day by day as you push yourself while coming up with jokes. In a similar way, becoming a writer is a process that happens over time as long as you honor the act of sitting down to write every day.

So how can you, however, maintain that consistency in striving for goals? How can you maintain your focus on the action rather than the end result?

Measuring your progress is the key.

Measure The Gain Rather Than The Gap

Too frequently, we gauge our level of accomplishment by comparing it to the goal we set for ourselves a year ago. We compare our current accomplishments with our ultimate goals.

This occurs frequently in real life. But as soon as we realize how far we still have to travel, a hybrid wave of pessimism and demotivation surges inside of us. You start to think, "All this work I've done and I'm still so far from where I want to be"

Funny how our minds can deceive us.

But as we are aware, how we think affects how we perceive the environment. The gap is the separation between where you are right now and where you want to go in the future. You'll keep seeing how far behind you are as long as you keep concentrating on that distance, which will make you feel discouraged about your efforts.

So how should progress be measured properly? Look behind you rather than ahead. Look backwards from where you are now to where you were in the beginning. Do you realize how far you've come? Do you recognize all the challenges you've overcome and raging rivers you've traversed? You have conquered a lot of doubts.

"The Gain" is the distance that has already been traveled; it is far more energizing, satisfying, and exciting than what lay in "The Gap."

Consider Your Progress Rather Than Your Ideals

The fact that "The Gap" will only get wider if you are completely focused on it has the unfortunate side effect of turning you into a rabbit in search of an elusive carrot.

How?

So take into account the fact that you are constantly evolving. You are constantly developing, changing, and learning. The person you were 10 years ago is not the same as the person you are today, and the same is true for the person you will be in five years.

Your ideals will evolve along with you as you continue to develop and change. You will outgrow your own principles just as you outgrow your own clothes. Your objectives and values will advance along with you as you move forward.

The important takeaway from this is that since your ideal is a continually shifting goal, anything you decide to pursue will constantly evade you.

Therefore, if you fall into the trap of comparing your present self to your *ideal* self, there will always be a gap to close and you will never be content with where you are right now. Additionally, you'll never feel deserving of yourself. In fact, it's advisable to concentrate on your progress rather than your ideal because of this. Your major metric for success should be the progress you've already made.

As a result, turn around and compare your current position to your starting place.

If you are in The Gain rather than The Gap, you will feel as though you have accomplished something wonderful. And it's the emotion that will silence your inner critic and push you on to continue.

Recognize your growth and how far you've come. Really, all it takes is one minute to change the way you think, many seconds to change the next course you pursue.

How to Track Your Progress

The ability to stay focused and persistent in carrying out your plans is what makes the difference between attaining your goals and failing to do so. This allows you to determine the effectiveness of your plans, and find new strategies to continue your progress if your original plans were lacking.

You can monitor your progress toward your goals in a variety of ways. Here are four methods you can employ to monitor your success in accomplishing goals.

Take a Broad Perspective

This is the cornerstone of tracking your growth and achieving your goals. Many of us simply go through the motions on a daily basis. We are not fully utilizing each day but are only in "survival mode."

Take a step back and consider the larger picture before you can begin tracking your development. Why do you behave in this way? What does it mean to start the day by waking up in the morning? Consider these factors and provide your responses with the goal in mind. In every area of your life, where do you picture yourself in the future?

Spend some time thinking about your objectives and imagining the larger picture. You need to look at the wider picture rather than merely going through the motions without purpose or inspiration.

Organize and Schedule Your Time

Planning and managing your time are essential to achieving your goals and keeping track of your progress in that direction. Once you understand the big picture, you then plan and coordinate the actions you must take to reach your objectives.

Take a look at your calendar and make a schedule that will allow you to accomplish all of your goals. A fantastic approach to keep track of your progress is by utilizing your phone, Google Calendar, or a planner. You'll set specific objectives for yourself each week.

In addition to feeling accomplished that you are making progress toward your goals, being able to plan and manage your time effectively helps you build important life skills like self-control, determination, growth mindset, and focus.

Search For Accountability

Tell your partner or a close friend about your aims. It's crucial that someone else check in with you on your development. You are more likely to finish your tasks throughout the week when someone other than yourself is holding you accountable. Both the desire to not let them down and the encouragement and support they provide when you do succeed in your aims will serve as motivation for you.

Celebrate Little Victories

It's crucial for you to pause after each accomplishment and recognize your success. You are more likely to burn out if you are always looking forward and never stop to appreciate your successes. Burnout makes it difficult to maintain concentration on your objectives.

Honoring your successes, no matter how modest, is a means for you to monitor your progress toward your objectives. Before moving on to your next objective, you'll be able to pause and acknowledge your diligence.

Be sure that you take the time and effort to celebrate any accomplishments.

Chapter 7:

A Work-Life Balance

A growth mindset is useful in the personal and professional life. Often-times, life can get in the way, and we have a hard time striking a balance between our personal and professional lives. This might cause conflict at work and even at home. But it is important that as growth-minded individuals, we make that distinct separation, while still balancing both lives.

In this chapter, we will focus on balancing work and personal life, while being the best at both, using a growth mindset.

On The Job

The main element that determines how we act and have an impact on people around us is our mindsets. This, too, has a significant impact on our professional lives as it does our personal lives.

So, what value does our mindset truly have on our careers?

The Usefulness of a Growth Mindset to Professional Life

Having a growth mindset is effective in every aspect of life, and this includes our professional lives. We know that having a growth mindset sets us apart from the average thinker, boosts productivity, and enhances the way we view life. Here are three ways that a growth mindset enhances our professional lives.

Increased Efficiency

The way we approach goals and react to effort and difficulty depends on our mindset. As a result, a team with growth mindsets may effectively encourage innovation and development—both for the organization and for one another.

For those who have a fixed mindset, their resistance to change may impede the organization's progress in terms of innovation. These people would be on the lookout for chances to showcase their abilities regularly (instead of learning). Additionally, they see trying out new duties as an opportunity to fail and put their professional performance in danger.

On the other hand, people with a growth mindset are always open to challenges and failures because they help them figure out where they went wrong and how to deal with failures so they can move on to success.

Improved Management

Managers who adopt a growth mindset greatly help their staff. Why? A manager who is focused on growth will be more receptive to suggestions and criticism from his staff without mistaking it for a criticism of their ability.

Because they believe that one's potential can be increased, managers with growth mindsets are stronger at approaching and directing people when it comes to coaching and mentoring.

Fixed-minded managers frequently hold fast to their initial opinions of their staff members. This means that if a manager thinks of a worker as a "high performer," he will hold onto that opinion even if the worker's performance declines.

In contrast, a growth-minded leader will pay more attention to how their team members evolve, therefore regardless of how they previously performed, both positive and negative changes will be recognized.

More Diversity

Organizations that support a growth culture are more receptive to creating a workforce that is inclusive and varied. Growth-minded leaders reject the idea of "fixed qualities." They therefore welcome anyone who is willing to continuously improve and offer value to the organization. Employees are also inspired to collaborate more when they work in a culture that values progress.

People with a fixed attitude frequently fall into stereotypes because they think that talent is something that one has forever. No matter what achievements a group of individuals actually has, stereotypes about them are easily established, especially when they come from underrepresented groups.

Self-Discipline and Professional Life

Professionals that have self-discipline develop productive practices that advance their careers. You require self-discipline to execute your everyday chores effectively regardless of your work or business.

What is Self-Discipline?

Self-discipline is a behavior that enables you to discover your abilities and conquer obstacles. You can concentrate intensively on a task or objective with the help of self-discipline in order to get the desired result. A number of additional characteristics, including ambition, desire, motivation, and responsibility, are frequently exhibited by people who are self-disciplined.

Why is Self-Discipline Important?

Self-discipline helps you to succeed in life. It holds you accountable for your goals and aids in the establishment of a regular work schedule.

Self-discipline also has the following advantages:

- **Increases your likelihood of moving up in your career**: Strong self-discipline enables you to visualize your objectives and create strategies for achieving them.

- **Reduces stress and anxiety levels**: You can stay on track with both your personal and professional goals if you have self-discipline.

- **Boosts your confidence and sense of self**: When your output increases, so do your confidence, happiness, and sense of self. Regularly achieving your goals gives you a sense of pride and self-confidence, which boosts your self-esteem.

- **Improves interpersonal and professional relationships**: Keeping track of tasks and objectives boosts your confidence and motivation, which you can transfer to others.

How to Develop Self-Discipline

Since developing self-discipline is a learned behavior, you should decide to do so. It's critical to have well-defined objectives and an effective plan for achieving them. It's simpler to maintain concentration and stay focused when you know where you're going. Here are some actions you can do to develop self-control:

- Determine your areas for development.
- Set expectations and objectives for yourself.
- Strive hard to achieve your objectives.
- Track your development.
- When you achieve goals, treat yourself.
- Take note of the circumstance.

Nine Professionalism Characteristics

What qualities will distinguish you as a professional? Let's examine nine essential traits:

Competence

Professionals get the job done well. You match your role's requirements and typically exceed expectations. However, you never push forward merely for show. Professionalism lets you manage your own as well as others' expectations and ask for help when needed.

Knowledge

Professionalism requires having specialized, up-to-date knowledge. You may master your role at every stage of your career and keep learning.

Additionally, it's crucial to put your knowledge to use. Being professional is showing what you know, not for self-promotion, but to help others achieve.

Conscientiousness

Professionalism means being reliable, setting high standards, and caring about your work. It also means being diligent, structured, and responsible for your thoughts, words, and deeds.

Conscientiousness isn't working longer hours or stressing over details. You should plan and prioritize your work and don't let perfectionism hold you back.

Integrity

Integrity keeps professionals honest. It prevents them from surrendering their ideals, even if it's difficult. Integrity means being honest with yourself and others. Everyone should see that your views and actions are genuine.

Professionalism is modeling courtesy and good manners for everyone, not just those you want to impress.

Respect

Being a professional requires modeling good manners and courtesy for everyone, not just those you need to impress. Additionally, by considering their needs and supporting the protection of their rights, you demonstrate your genuine regard for other people.

Emotional Intelligence

Being a true professional requires maintaining your composure under pressure. This requires emotional intelligence and empathy for others.

Professionalism occasionally entails controlling your emotions. However, there are other occasions when it's crucial to express your emotions in order to engage in meaningful conversations or defend your beliefs.

Time Management

Being able to manage time effectively is another key trait of being professional. With both work and home life, professionals should be able to strike a balance with their times, while avoiding burn out.

Appropriateness

Professionals know what's proper in particular scenarios. It prevents awkwardness, enhances credibility, and gives you role security. Appropriateness also includes attire, grooming, and body language. It includes how you speak, write, and conduct with others.

Confidence

Well-founded confidence reassures and drives others, strengthening your impact and leadership. It motivates you to take on new tasks because you don't worry about hurting your reputation. Professionalism makes you confident in what you're doing but ready to improve and do more.

The Importance of Working Well With Others

Being able to effectively work with others is a virtue that is generally acknowledged. Having a growth mindset leaves you open and receptive to the ideas and input of others, while working productively and avoiding conflict.

Conflict between partners or coworkers often surfaces due to barriers in conversation, being unable to exercise emotional intelligence and misconceptions. However, teamwork is a wonderful aspect of any workplace, and having a growth mindset should help in overcoming these barriers, and putting our best forward with our teams, in order to achieve our goals.

Effective Work Is Done in Teams

Employee collaboration empowers your staff to:

- Break up challenging projects into simpler ones, then collaborate to finish them more quickly.

- Develop specialized abilities to enable the right individual for each activity to complete it more quickly and effectively.

In a nutshell, teams increase productivity. Better productivity, lower expenses, higher profitability, and a host of other advantages may result from this.

Teams Self-Report

When one person completes a task alone, they have complete liberty, but who will correct them if they begin to work slowly or ineffectively?

In a team effort, multiple people are accountable for the same objective. Most importantly, teammates evaluate and rely on the caliber of one another's work. W

Teams Invent More Quickly

There are generally innumerable answers for any activity or issue. When a team works on an issue, the project gains from a variety of viewpoints, expertise, and experiences at once.

Therefore, a team approach can result in quicker, more profound innovation.

Teammates Benefit From One Another

As teams cooperate, they will quickly discover each other's strengths and rectify one other's errors. Furthermore, everyone's performance will rise.

Teamwork Can Foster Constructive Competition

The performance of a team can keep getting better as long as the correct challenges and incentives are in place to encourage competitiveness.

Teamwork Fosters Enduring Business Partnership

Employees develop ties that can develop into trust and camaraderie when they work as a team and achieve. Additionally, it's beneficial for your company since staff members who get along well with one another are more likely to:

- Clearly communicate with one another.
- Encourage and support one another.
- Cooperative work.

Your Inner Circle

Our life cannot exist without relationships, but they also carry with them both great splendors and dreadful sights. Evenings of joy spent with others might be marred by intense resentment.

However, by insulting or disparaging a friend or family member who has offended or hurt you, we may unintentionally increase their bad effects. These responses frequently result from a lack of hope—the conviction that the offender can improve or learn from this mistake.

Growth mindsets, or simply the notion that one may learn from failure, can be applied to both our personal life and our interpersonal relationships. We can decide to take advantage of these opportunities to right a wrong, express hurt, promote change for the better, and strengthen relationships.

How we respond to people can be significantly influenced by our growth attitude. We confront others with hope and love rather than rage and resentment.

We can apply this growth mindset to our interpersonal relationships in the same way that we try to learn from our own mistakes. Maybe we can make beauty out of a show.

To encourage a growth mindset in relationships, for example you may do the following:

- Be adaptable to change and the idea that healthy relationships occasionally call for review and tweaking.

- Even if it makes you uncomfortable, be open to hearing and comprehending the various requirements in a partnership.

- Recognize that understanding, clarifying, and respecting our partner's opinions or wants does not need us to agree with them or to forego our own.

Through persistent efforts of contemplation and regular communication between partners, you can build a loving relationship.

Everyone is unique. Everyone has diverse life experiences. Even if we can't always meet everyone's requirements, both parties' needs and opinions are important in every relationship. Be sure to practice respect, loyalty, comprise, and honesty by doing the following:

- Every day or week, show each other your respect and appreciation in sweet and simple ways that show how much you care.

- Avoid taking things personally, but make an effort to have an unbiased viewpoint on the topic at hand. The common ground can then start to show itself.

- Wait until everyone has calmed down before engaging in a serious conversation. Never be reluctant to put a conversation on hold and resume it later.

- Be willing to learn from criticism. Instead of being a command or demand for change, let it serve as a benchmark.

Whether we like it or not, discomfort and pain accompany growth. If you don't want to change, you could not get much further in life. We must constantly remind ourselves that developing a growth mindset in our relationships is never too late. We might decide to adopt a growth mindset in order to create those amazing moments with the significant people in our lives.

With a firm belief in openness, growth, willingness, love, and care, may we all be able to tell a story of love that is filled with various color spectrums emerging from continual conversations and reflections in relationships.

Fixed Mindsets in Relationships

People with the fixed mindset have a propensity to anticipate everything positive to occur spontaneously and automatically, which is dangerous. They are compelled to believe that this would magically happen through their love, rather than building the basis of their relationship on working together to help one another handle their difficulties and develop their talents.

The fixed mindset believes that an ideal couple should be able to read each other's minds and complete each other's words, which can dangerously lead to the false notion that couples, families or friends can read each other's minds. Even if it's genuinely delightful to imagine, it might lead to inflated expectations, which strengthens the stuck mindset's grip.

No great accomplishment has ever been achieved without failure, and the same is true for great relationships. People with a fixed attitude place blame when they discuss their disagreements. While they frequently blame their relationship, they also occasionally blame themselves. And they place blame on a characteristic.

But things don't stop there. Because it's in their nature to think that a person's traits are fixed and unchangeable, people with fixed mindsets feel entitled to be angry and disgusted with their partners when they blame their partner's personality for the issue. These characteristics are anchored, making them unchangeable. It creates a never-ending cycle that feeds hatred and sadness into such relationships.

Our mental models are always changing. The person we are today is a combination of the lingering effects of our upbringing, the inner child within us, and the mature mind we have developed over time. To make an effort to change our thoughts, we must confront and gradually overcome our ingrained biases. It will be difficult, time-consuming, and painful. But the growth mindset actually teaches us that.

So, rather than aiming for perfection, the goal should be continuous improvement and joint growth motivated by love.

Water and Oil?

Despite the many advantages, finding a healthy balance between your personal and professional life can be difficult. You can improve this fragile balance between professional and private interests for more pleasure and personal fulfillment by employing particular tactics.

What Does Balancing Work and Life Mean?

Work-life balance involves adjusting priorities and attention between personal and professional duties. Adjusting your timing helps you distribute your mental capacity and concentration equally.

Work-Life Balance Advantages

Several advantages of living a balanced life include the following:

Happiness and Satisfaction Increase

Personal and professional balance increases pleasure and contentment. You have more freedom to pursue the priorities that are most important to you since only a small portion of your attention is focused in one area. A balanced existence allows time for personal relationships, interests, and physical wellness.

Personal and Professional Relationships Improved

Work-life balance improves professional and personal relationships. Spending too much time on work means less time with family and friends. When you have a better life balance, you can improve your relationships. Then, you're happier and more fulfilled with your personal life. This improves your quality of life and career.

Productivity Increases

When you're balanced, you're more productive and efficient. Life balance improves mental and physical health, boundaries, and time to ponder and process information. This might help you focus on the task at hand and boost your productivity.

Accept That No Perfect Balance Exists

People often try to balance personal and professional life. There's no one method to balance life. Work and life priorities will always fluctuate, so remain flexible throughout your days, weeks, and months. Sometimes work takes priority over personal life. Sometimes personal life trumps work.

Accept that your life's balance is always altering, and you'll be happier. Instead of ideal balance, aim for realism. With time and knowledge, you'll create a balanced life.

Embrace Imperfection

When managing life, give up perfectionism. Perfectionism causes professional burnout and job stress. Focus on accomplishment and production, not perfectionism. Giving up on perfectionism encourages creativity and flow, resulting in improved work quality and personal pleasure.

Reduce Time-Wasting

Identify your personal and professional priorities when managing your life. Knowing your priorities and values helps you stay focused on what is important. Once you know your priorities, you can focus on tasks that advance your goals. This reduces time-wasting tasks that can divert your attention.

Disconnect

Remembering to switch off your computer and unplug is crucial to greater life balance. This is vital for remote and home-based workers. It's tempting to get caught up in the ability to work at all hours, but there are also negatives.

Turn off your computer daily. If this isn't possible, set your computer notifications to switch off at the end of the workday to reduce personal distractions.

Scheduling

Review your calendar to improve work-life balance. Adjust your professional and personal schedules to attain balance. If you have a big project due at work, you may need to rearrange your schedule to accommodate longer hours. Flexibility, time management, and delegation help improve work-life balance.

Stress-Reduction Approaches

Unbalanced professional and personal lives might increase stress. To overcome this strain, adopt proper stress management. Add exercise to your everyday routine, eat healthy wholesome meals at home, or go to bed early to prepare for a meeting. Try meditation, breathing techniques, or gentle yoga. A lunchtime walk might help you decompress and re-energize for the afternoon.

In the end, having a growth mindset requires balance, contentment, and effectiveness. Hence, our aim should be to achieve this.

Chapter 8:

Speed Bumps and Roadblocks

Mistakes, failures and setbacks happen, but the person with a growth mindset owns up, takes responsibility, and moves forward. In this chapter, we will focus on how you might achieve this.

Everyone Fails

When someone says, "Failure is not an option" don't listen to them. Of course, there might be a certain definition to their perception of failure. Perhaps they mean "failing and staying down" isn't an option. But 'failure' in its own sense, can and most definitely will be an option.

Benefits of Failure

Those with a growth mindset actually welcome failure since it helps them to do just that: grow.

So, failure is okay, and here's why.

It's Unavoidable

You'll fail once in your life. Talent, intellect, work and effort, and/or passion won't help. Unavoidable failure.

Failure is a given but don't be duped by it. Some of the most successful persons of our time have failed, too. Failure helped Steve Jobs, Oprah Winfrey, Milton Hershey, and Walt Disney become successful. So, relax. You're among legends.

Failure Is The Best Teacher

Even the best of people can improve. Failure can reveal which areas need work. Like job training, your supervisor may point up errors when you first start. This is meant to help, not discourage. Next time, you'll know what to do. Instead of moping after a setback, ask, "What did I do wrong?" Next time, you can fix the problem and do better.

Fear of Failure Leads to Lessens Opportunities

Fearful people are dull. They don't ever take risks. People who are unafraid if failure go for the big things, even when success isn't sure or even realistic. They'll enter a musical even though they can't sing. Even if they don't qualify, they'll apply for the big job. These risks enhance life.

Failure Strengthens

Failure divides weak and strong. Some fail and quit, while others fail and gain invincibility. These people can be knocked down, but they bounce right back. It should motivate you to pursue your ambitions… again. If you can survive this, you can withstand anything.

Failure Sweetens Triumph

How can you know success without failure? After repeatedly failing, eventually succeeding is a great feeling. You'll feel satisfied knowing everything was worth it.

How to Accept Failure and Use It to Your Advantage

Managing failure in the workplace and life requires effort, acceptance, and movement. Here are some pointers for transforming failure into success:

Don't Sit There and Think About It

Take into account other possibilities and take steps to address the issue you encountered. When something goes wrong, working to fix it as opposed to obsessing on it can frequently help you become more motivated and succeed more quickly.

Distinguish Failing From Failure

Many people distinguish between failing and failure, viewing failing as the attempt to try something that you later discover doesn't work and failure as the act of giving up and quitting. You can maintain your drive for success by separating the phrases.

Consider Failure to Be a Tool

Think about adjusting your perspective on failure and using it as a tool to assist you figure out what works and what doesn't. You can accept and benefit from failure if you see it as a chance to innovate rather than as a barrier to success.

Determine What Success Means to You

Understanding what you want to accomplish and how you define success can also assist you in determining failure and how to overcome it.

Keep It Professional

Consider maintaining a professional tone and exercising emotional intelligence since how you respond to a failure or error in a professional context frequently matters more than the mistake itself. Maintain your composure, awareness, and comprehension of the issue.

After a Break, Make New Goals

After failing, taking a break might help you put the experience in perspective and determine what lessons can be drawn from it. After that, think about organizing yourself and concentrating on the subsequent steps toward attaining your initial intended outcome or a new victory. Set precise targets and consider developing an action plan.

Owning Up

Owning your mistakes is frequently a sign of professionalism and maturity, both of which are essential traits for a growth mindset and success.

We all err from time to time. Sometimes the mistake is rather small, such as a few typos in a report. Other times, it's a bigger error, like losing a crucial client. Even while it's natural to want to blame yourself, someone else or even come up with an explanation for why it occurred, there is only one thing you can do to move on constructively: accept responsibility for your mistakes.

Why Owning Your Mistakes Has Advantages

Making a mistake is unpleasant, but if you don't act appropriately, it might grow much worse. For instance, if you continually criticize yourself, it will be difficult for you to move on. Even some of your confidence can be lost. On the other hand, if you routinely try to transfer the blame somewhere else, it may lead to conflict at work or in your personal relationships.

Additionally, when you accept responsibility for your mistakes, you show honesty and accountability. Your boss, coworkers, friends, schoolmates or family can tell that you are trustworthy and willing to accept responsibility for your activities. They'll probably respect you more as a result of that. They'll also be more willing to assist you in fixing your errors so you can use them as teaching points.

How to Accept Responsibility For Your Mistakes

So how do you go about taking responsibility for your mistakes?

The following steps are involved in owning a mistake:

- **Acknowledge your mistake:** To put it another way, don't dodge it. It's ideal if you catch your error before someone else does. Although, that is not to say that you should hide your mistakes from others, or deny it if someone else points it out.

- **Make an action plan**: Determine how to fix the error so it fulfills the promise as closely as possible. If you've missed a deadline, for instance, think about how quickly you can deliver.

- **Inform the individuals who will be harmed by the mistake**: This might be the hardest. However, inform your manager, teammates, friends, and your coworkers of the mistake. It's advisable to refrain from giving specifics unless they specifically want them because doing so may come off as you are offering justifications.

- **Get a solution**: Tell them about your alternative approach and ask if they are satisfied. If not, talk about alternative solutions until you find one that appeals to all parties.

- **Carry through**: It's crucial to put a plan into action once one has been chosen in order to avoid disappointment again. Ask for help if you require it.

Since nobody is perfect, you will occasionally make mistakes. They can, however, help you develop into a more regarded, trustworthy, and resourceful person, student or worker if you own up to them and take the proper corrective action.

Spring In My Step

Acceptance is a little representation of who we are, where our values, attitudes, and actions cast a radiant glow of optimism. We all know what it's like to be downcast or disheartened because of the challenges of maintaining optimism in this era of easily accessible discouragement.

When we evaluate our thoughts or emotions through the prism of self-judgment and prior sorrow, our mood changes. We can't control every emotion, but acceptance can indirectly affect them.

The fundamental skill of acceptance requires us to accept anything that may occur, even if it is bad. It is challenging to accept something we find to be painful, risky, or destructive, despite the fact that acceptance is different from approval or agreement.

True acceptance is a sort of forgiveness because it chooses peace over chaos. It's letting go of pain we can't control. Oftentimes we resist reality because we don't know alternative options. But when we accept reality, we have calmer thoughts and clearer motivations. We've stopped fighting "what is," therefore we have more energy and passion for life.

Acceptance reduces resistance to "what is," that is, what has already happened and what we can't necessarily change. This, in turn allows greater relationships, more creativity, and healthier attitudes.

A pleasant chain reaction of beneficial outcomes can be produced by seeing our experiences from the perspective of receptiveness and acceptance.

Acceptance's Healing Power

When life seems difficult, our need for empathetic acceptance is most apparent.

To go ahead in a state of peace, we require the therapeutic power of total forgiveness. By expressing your feelings, you'll be able to feel them and so be able to overcome them, breaking the hold of denial.

Only then can our soul's voice pinpoint the source of our displeasure. So, acceptance restores the soul.

Accepting your mishaps and failures is an act of self-love, forgiveness, empathy, and acceptance. Fighting truth is exhausting and ineffective; it keeps us entrenched in old routines, beliefs, and harmful situations.

Acceptance Encourages Growth

For those with a growth mindset, you might want to acknowledge the power of acceptance to growth. Accepting life's challenges and failures can be tiring, but it is necessary for growth.

By avoiding life's unpleasantness, we limit our ability for compassion and add unnecessary uneasiness.

Oh No! Not Again!

Maybe you've failed before, and the thought of it happening again makes you shiver. But fear of failing might overshadow motivation to succeed. Insecurity causes many people to unknowingly hinder their success.

In this section, we'll also discuss ways to overcome fear of failure for career and personal success.

What Is Fear of Failing

Failure-related fear will make you steer clear of potentially hazardous situations.

Fear of failure prevents you from trying again, fosters self-doubt, halts development, and may tempt you to act unethically, for example, cheating.

Here are some ways that being fearful of failing can slow you down:

- You might lose chances in life.

- Your creativity might decline.

- High achievers can lose out on further opportunities.

Overcoming Fear of Failure (Step-By-Step)

It's typically okay to be afraid of failing. I mean, who *likes* to fail? Still, your fear shouldn't be crippling, and it should be more of motivation not to fail a second or third time, rather than an aspect that holds you back. Growth-minded people know that failure doesn't have to be a bad thing. So here are a few steps to overcoming fear of failing:

Discover The Source of The Fear

Consider the source of your negative belief. Write down the source of your worry and make an effort to understand it from an outsider's perspective. Perhaps a traumatic event from your youth or a long-standing insecurity are the causes of your worry. By identifying the root of the fear, some of its strength is diminished.

Reframe Your Goal-Related Beliefs

Sometimes having an all or nothing mindset leaves you with nothing. Have a clear idea of what you want to achieve, but make learning something new a part of it. You have a significantly lower chance of failing if you consistently strive for growth and learning.

Visualize Outcomes

Uncertainty is scary .Spend some time considering the potential effects of your choice. Consider best and worst case scenarios. If you've had a chance to psychologically get ready for what can occur, you'll feel better.

Practice Positivity

You frequently believe the things you tell yourself. How you respond and act is influenced by your self-talk.

Negative self-talk and triggers are your responsibility. Replace negative thinking with good thoughts. You can build mental scripts to use when negativity strikes. Your inner voice affects your actions.

Look at The Worst-Case Scenario

Sometimes, the worst-case scenario could be utterly disastrous. But when horrible things happen, they frequently don't mean the end of everything beautiful.

It's critical to consider how awful the worst-case situation would be in the overall context of your life. We occasionally give situations more authority than they merit. A failure is usually not irreparable.

Plan Ahead

We've probably heard "Hope for the best, plan for the worst" once or twice before, and it is sound advice. A backup plan never hurts. If the worst happens, you shouldn't scramble for a solution. You are more likely to move forward and take reasonable risks if you have a backup plan.

Having a backup is a fantastic approach to decrease anxiety about failure.

Whatever Occurs, Learn From It

Something not going as planned doesn't necessarily mean you've failed. Whatever happens, learn from it. Even a bad situation can be a chance to grow.

In essence, failing isn't something we might always embrace, but it is a part of life. We should always be open and receptive to accepting, embracing and learning from mistakes, failures and setbacks as we train to establish a growth mindset. Because in the end, the ultimate goal is, indeed, to grow.

Chapter 9:

There's Always Something New

Learning is a never-ending process and people with growth mindsets make use of every opportunity to gain new knowledge, accept good advice and step out of their comfort zones.

In this penultimate chapter, we will talk about the importance of continuously building on your knowledge and being open to learning new things, as well as how you can achieve this.

Willing to Learn

Keeping your knowledge and abilities up to date will help you advance your career and life. Professional and personal development should be a focus, whether it's learning new technologies or improving emotional intelligence. In today's competitive corporate world, it helps you stand out. Having a growth mindset requires content and effectiveness. learning. And no, this doesn't mean that you should have your nose in a book 24/7 as if you're studying for a middle school mid-term exam. But keeping your skills sharp and constantly learning is vital to a growth mindset.

Here are eight strategies to keep updating your knowledge and skills.

Take Development Courses

Expanding your professional skill set, learning something new, or even earning academic credit toward a degree are all possible outcomes of taking professional development courses. Online courses are flexible and inexpensive. Before paying, examine instructor profiles, reviews, and the curriculum. Additionally, vendor-taught workshops, universities, and training institutes also offer professional development courses.

Use Web Resources

The Internet provides unlimited free information and learning resources. Attend webinars, follow industry experts' blogs or social media, or bookmark industry news sites and web forums to keep current. Sign up for news notifications or an RSS feed like Feedly.com to keep track of industry news. It doesn't even have to be related to your work. You can generally follow anything of interest to you.

Attend Events

Professional, academic and informing events are great for learning and growth. Local enterprises, schools, non-profit organizations, government agencies, business groups, and professional associations organize seminars, forums, and workshops for the public sometimes. Consider these events as networking opportunities to share ideas with peers who can offer fresh perspectives.

Online Networking

In this every growing and changing world, you realize the value of creating and maintaining a contact list. Use LinkedIn to connect with company executives, social media to market your business or brand, network with professionals, and stay in touch with clients.

Connect with friends and followers on Facebook; network creatively and share news on Twitter, or blog to increase your online credibility and establish relationships with potential clients and those you can constantly learn from.

Get Certification or Further Your Education

Continuing education and qualification programs can increase reliability and reflect a dedication to your profession. Learning a new software application before it becomes mainstream, committing to industry benchmarks through a certification program, or keeping up with market trends by taking a class can boost your income and position you competitively in your field. Also, if you have an interest that you'd like to explore, you can get certification in this field, and perhaps even monetize yourself! For example, if you like to write, you can take online creative writing courses, and maybe one day, publish our book.

Learn From Others

Thought leaders can share essential knowledge, thoughts, and guidance on social media. Follow individuals in your verticals and in skill areas you have or wish to build. By reading regular pieces, you can not only gain knowledge, but also establish relationships by responding and sharing their content. You can even learn from those around you who you know. Surround yourself with skilled, motivated people.

Read Case Studies and Research Papers

Top enterprises, consulting firms, schools, agencies, and think tanks often issue research papers and case studies on industry trends and studies. Use these resources to improve your knowledge.

Read Widely

When I was in university, my professors always told us to "read widely." At the time, it was bugging, but the truth is, it's sound advice. Reading is a wonderful way to keep gaining knowledge. Non-fiction books, articles, blogs and random posts are always available, and keeps your mind sharp and receptive to always learning.

Be Able to Take Criticism

No matter how it's presented, criticism can be difficult to give or receive. However, offering and receiving constructive criticism is key to growth. It can assist us in generating greater results, discover motivation, and enhance connections when presented effectively.

What is Constructive Criticism?

Constructive criticism is straightforward, truthful, and simple to apply. It offers concrete illustrations and solutions for effective positive change. This kind of criticism also identifies areas where the recipient can enhance their conduct to reduce potential issues in the future.

Benefits of Constructive Criticism

Constructive criticism fosters trust and offers room for improvement on both sides. Context and practical guidance are two essential components of constructive criticism.

This feedback gives the recipient information around their improvement areas, which is vital for understanding why feedback is being delivered.

Providing concrete suggestions and actions to support the added context can help to increase mutual trust. This enables communication, collaboration, and career development.

Receiving Constructive Criticism

How do you handle criticism? Can you accept suggestions without being defensive?

It can be difficult to take criticism from a coworker, a friend, or someone you don't fully trust. But it's important to keep in mind that unbiased, constructive criticism can often originate from unreliable sources.

Here's a 5-step approach for accepting criticism gracefully:

- **Don't react immediately**: Remain composed and avoid any reaction at all. Remain composed at all times. Then, you can try to understand your critic's motivation and perception.

- **Listen carefully**: Listen to the other person's thoughts and views.

- **Show gratitude**. You don't have to agree with the feedback, but showing gratitude shows you appreciate your colleagues' or friend's efforts.

- **Ask questions and express your perspective**: Ask for specific examples, acknowledge non-disputable feedback, and request solutions.

- **Follow up:** If it's a major concern, request a follow-up appointment to ask more questions and discuss future steps. This pause allows you to analyze feedback, seek counsel, and brainstorm solutions. Ideally, you'll also say what you'll do next and thank the person again.

Five Mistakes to Avoid When Accepting Criticism

Don't ignore or disregard criticism that is offered in a constructive manner. A reputable, unbiased source's opinion about your work, management style, or appearance is invaluable.

Avoid these five reactions to receiving *constructive* criticism:

- Avoid becoming defensive and angry in your response.

- Don't criticize the person who provided the feedback.

- Don't talk over or interrupt the individual who is providing the feedback.

- Do not first analyze or challenge the person's assessment.

- Avoid having a discussion or responding in a hostile manner.

Destructive Criticism

Destructive criticism is directed at someone with the goal to cause them harm or offend. We should know when someone is trying to tear us down, or truly trying to help.

Here are a few ways to distinguish destructive and constructive criticism:

- **Intention**: Constructive criticism helps a person better his work, while negative criticism hurts and embarrasses him.

- **Areas criticized**: Instead of focusing on the work, destructive critique may highlight flaws in the creator's strengths and limitations.

- **Critic**: Experts in the topic are individuals who provide constructive criticism, whilst those who provide destructive criticism are not very informed on the subject.

- **Help**: Destructive critique doesn't give improvement suggestions.

- **Nature of feedback**: Contrary to destructive criticism, constructive criticism is explicit, unambiguous, and actionable.

Always try to disregard damaging criticism and not become irritated or wounded by it.

Out Of My Comfort Zone

Opportunities to venture outside of one's comfort zone are abundant in life, but seizing them can be challenging.

Sometimes the issue is a lack of understanding of the benefits. After all, why would we try to give up the luxury of comfort? More often than not, people are held back by this portrayal of a fixed mindset.

Moving From The Comfort to The Growth Zone

To leave your comfort zone and enter the growth zone requires guts. It is impossible to improve upon prior experiences without a clear route map. This might make you feel anxious.

It's vital to note, however, that similar to other attempts at behavioral modification, entering the growth zone is more difficult without some degree of self-awareness.

The transition from a comfort zone to a growth zone can't be straightforward. Peaks, valleys, and plateaus can make the trek more challenging. In other cases, we may need to occasionally withdraw to our familiar surroundings before gathering the fortitude to venture out again. Even so, accepting the process might make uncertainty easier to bear.

It's alluring to feel secure, in charge, and that things are going smoothly when you are in your comfort zone. However, the best sailors aren't necessarily born in calm waters.

Benefits of Leaving Your Comfort Zone

Leaving your comfort zone has many rewards beyond performance. Here are four general examples:

Growth-Mindset

With a fixed mindset, people feel they have distinct doses of each ability and an achievement ceiling. Hence, failure and criticism may destroy self-esteem.

However, the growth mindset is adaptable. Setbacks become learning opportunities, and our potential grows.

Developing a growth mindset requires leaving your comfort zone. The fixed mindset traps us in dread of failure, but the growth mindset expands possibilities. It encourages learning and healthy risk-taking, leading to excellent life outcomes.

Self-Actualization

Self-actualization helps many leave their comfort zone. Abraham Maslow's (1943) theory of human motivation popularized the concept: "What a man can be, he must be. This need we may call self-actualization." Maslow's hierarchy of needs is a ladder, with basic and psychological requirements satisfying the comfort zone. Whether we realize it or not, we need personal progress and fulfillment.

This change is comparable to trying to achieve self-actualization as long as the choice to leave one's comfort zone is in line with one's values. Why is this crucial? Because failing to grow could result in immobility later in life.

Adaptability and Antifragility

Perhaps since life isn't exactly a predictable event, neither should people. Everyone encounters difficulties. But extending our comfort zone makes us more resilient to change and ambiguity.

Increased Self-confidence

Self-efficacy is the belief that one can accomplish goals. Goals that increase self-efficacy are particular, manageable, and time-bound.

Leaving your comfort zone entails a period of trial and error, during which success is likely to occur to some extent. When we achieve achievement, our self-efficacy and confidence in our abilities increases.

Although this won't happen overnight, like other comfort-zone benefits, accomplishment and confidence can be a powerful asset for anyone.

Seven Ways to Leave Your Comfort Zone

Let's discuss seven strategies to leave your comfort zone now that we've covered the what and why:

Change Routines

Everyday life is full of challenges. For example, turn off your phone and TV while eating, brush your teeth after getting dressed, and walk more slowly. You are forced out of your old, cozy habits by these changes.

Be Skeptical

While considering opposing viewpoints might be unsettling, doing so fosters development and understanding by uprooting long-held assumptions. This can be done by reading other genres, talking to new people, and traveling. Being trapped in our routines can lead to complacency—a comfort zone trait.

Step Up Your Fitness Game

Many also strive toward this objective. Some people may define it as finishing their first 5K, while others might define it as doing a triathlon.

Leaving your comfort zone through exercise is a terrific way to start.

Get a Diet Change

Many wish to change their diets and quit eating "comfort foods." This implies attempting new things. Sticking to a balanced diet can be difficult yet gratifying, and self-efficacy grows as you reach milestones.

Develop Your Skills

Skills development boosts creativity, self-confidence, and employability. Many people struggle with public speaking, negotiating, and leadership. Investing in them can generate resilience, satisfaction, and possibilities.

Be Honest

Honesty can encourage human growth when used sensitively. Being honest with yourself or a close friend takes you out of your comfort zone. We can better understand ourselves and others through honest conversation.

Recognizing and grabbing opportunities to leave your comfort zone isn't always easy. Hence, it's important to develop a growth-oriented mindset. This includes believing you're adaptive, reframing stress, and enduring worries and doubts.

Everyone must choose, intentionally or not. You can settle for what's comfortable and safe, or, you might be open to growth chances, challenging the status quo and exploring what you can do.

This behavior has lifelong benefits. We avoid disappointments and regrets and fulfill our full potential, in turn inspiring others.

Chapter 10:

The Domino Effect

Having a growth mindset means you see the importance of sharing what you know so that others can improve as well. We sometimes have a notion that success is rival and excludable, and helping others will mean there's less for you. But let's bust that myth and understand that we can share the knowledge of developing a growth mindset and that can ultimately help guide us to our success.

In this final chapter, we will talk about helping others develop a growth mindset, and how important it is to do this.

Enough to Go Around

Our world is a vast mine of infinite resources, that we, as humans, can never truly deplenish. So, thinking that success is reserved for some persons, while others should stand on the sidelines and wait for their shot, this doesn't have to be so.

The truth is, we all have our success already locked away in our minds, and that is the true importance of a growth mindset. When we have a mindset like this, absolutely nothing or no one will be able to take that from us, and so, our success is inevitable. And 'success' doesn't have to mean a million dollars a month, five mansions, and a hell of a tesla parked in your garage; it can mean something as simple as achieving your one year goal.

So, why do you think that if someone else gets a chance that you want, you can't also receive that chance? Or if someone succeeds to the degree you desire, does it mean you won't too?

It seems as though there is not enough for everyone.

However, success is the size of the ocean, not the size of a swimming pool. If someone is brave enough, there is a place for everyone who wants to jump into the waves.

On the sand, some individuals will assert that the ocean is the length of a swimming pool, criticizing the swimsuits of others, and comparing how some people are swimming elegantly while others are treading water. They constantly wish they had the courage to face the waters. There is no upper limit of 30 guests. No lifeguard is on duty. Although the waves can occasionally knock you about, you are always welcome to enter the ocean.

There is enough success for all of us to swim in, and we can even encourage others to do the same because the water is perfectly safe.

Each of us has a unique life map and has taken a unique trip. While we occasionally move in the same direction as other people for extended periods of time, we never, ever take their exact same steps.

Additionally, there are instances when we are too preoccupied with their achievement to even recognize that we are not always moving in the same direction as them. Instead of concentrating on the direction we are traveling in, we are more interested in what they are receiving that we are not.

Your abilities, words, aspirations, and desires are completely original to you.

Own your true differences and how awesome that is. When you feel jealous of someone else's success, remember how fiercely unique you are too and embrace how special they are.

Thus, there is no doubt that there's enough to last us a lifetime, and for others as well. So, helping someone achieve their own growth mindset for their success is not only important to the sustainability and productivity of those around you, but it is generally kind and gives you a sense of fulfillment in the end.

All Ships Are Lifted by a High Tide

If you are close to someone whose achievement is causing a high tide, you will inevitably be hoisted up with them. It doesn't always have to be a reflection of your own accomplishments. On the other hand, if someone you're with succeeds, you all get to celebrate it together. Positive energy feeds off of itself. Either you join the celebration or you can withdraw to a quiet spot and think about yourself.

It's impossible to see every action someone has taken. And it's likely that you wouldn't want to or be willing to follow their example.

Success rarely follows a straight line. We sometimes focus on someone else's arrival rather than their journey there. Some of the steps they had to take were uncomfortable, unattractive, and downright unpleasant. Don't simply focus on where someone arrived; consider all the steps they took to get there and keep in mind that you couldn't see them all.

Let's all remember to jump in and admire how wonderful the water feels.

Passing The Baton

Say, for instance, you have developed your growth mindset, and you have achieved your success. What do you do now? You can either continue to grow, help otters achieve this, or simply do both. As we previously established, achieving a growth mindset and success is enough for everyone. So, don't keep it to yourself! Share with someone else.

But how do you start to help improve the lives of others while assisting them in realizing their full potential and developing a right mindset?

In order to finally raise the individuals around you, it is crucial to inspire, empower, and support them throughout the process. Here are the seven E's for assisting others to develop a growth mindset and reaching their highest potential.

Engage

To be an effective influencer on others, take them on walks with them, and allow them to enjoy each step. This can be metaphorical or literal. Anything that facilitates communication and enables us to interact with others is a positive move to helping others develop a growth mindset. Why? Being interactive and engaging helps to build skill even without a lot of effort or intention.

Educate

The goal should be to enable others to reach their full potential through a growth mindset. It has teaching or mentoring as its cornerstone. We can adopt a hands-on, one-on-one strategy and mentor individuals rather than merely saying a few uplifting words, leaving them with no idea how to actually apply this to their lives.

Equip

Mentors should establish the parameters and criteria for a task, project, and regularly revise the vision, and then they give everyone else or even a single person with the resources they need to do their tasks and, eventually, complete their purpose.

Encourage

The motivation behind our attempts to engage, educate, and equip is encouragement. A healthy amount of encouragement helps to smooth out the rough edges. Good meteors and leaders show concern. If you have a calling to lead—and we are all called to lead in some way—then you have a calling to encourage.

Empower

It's time to release the people you mentor once they're prepared. But not until they are prepared. You must first engage, educate, equip, and encourage them as a mentor before doing so at other appropriate times. You can't just jump and empower them. For example, a school coach will make sure his teams are well-prepared so he wouldn't have to constantly instruct them while they are playing. In moments of need, he was there to offer advice and support, but he had prepared them so well that, once the game had begun, he was certain that his players would be able to perform on their own.

Energize

Good mentors motivate and inspire people. They seek out strategies to energize and excite others around them despite the challenges and stresses they personally experience every day.

Elevate

You must conduct yourself like a leader or mentor with your goals and the goals of others in mind. But your ultimate goal should be lifting up those you help or mentor, so one day, they can do the same for others as well. Elevating others can be hard, especially if you are not ready to let them go and watch them spread their wings. But if one person, starting with you, can help another reach their full potential, through a growth mindset, imagine the type of world we can build.

Being The Change

Every action and word we take has an impact on the people we care about, either favorably or unfavorably. The optimum way to approach this is with thought and purpose. Here are some ways you can help others to see and embrace their best selves, while being a mentor or role model.

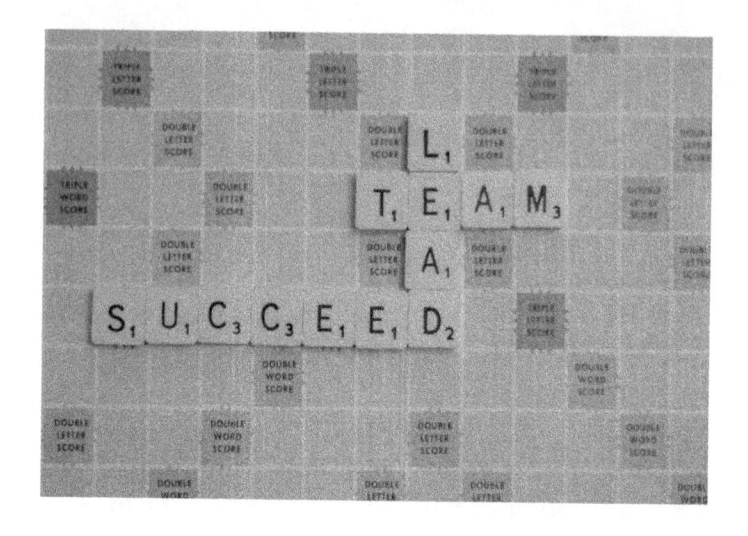

Hope For Them

We all experience self-doubt occasionally. We lack the confidence in our abilities to pursue a significant promotion or start a new project. In these circumstances, having somebody else believe in you is priceless.

Plan For It

It's common advice to avoid getting too hopeful. We are urged to set realistic goals for ourselves. But sometimes we have to raise our standards in order to support people in performing at their best. Although this can be overdone, there are numerous instances where a teacher, parent, or even a boss has asked us to do more than we had anticipated. And since we accepted the challenge, it gave us the ability to look farther than before.

Share The Truth

And do so with empathy. We frequently refrain from speaking the harsh reality out of fear of upsetting anyone. We strive to be kind. However, being honest is a sign of love. You might be the only one who will or can speak what needs to be said to someone else.

Act as a Model

Our behavior is one of the best methods to influence others. Our actions speak louder than our words do. Do not assume that someone is not observing you. They do. And they are both consciously and unconsciously taking note of everything about you. We unconsciously imitate our heroes. And since *everyone* looks up to us, let's all set positive examples.

Disclose Yourself

We overlook the need to admit our faults far too frequently. We hold back because we don't want to appear weak. By doing this, we rob others of our knowledge, humanity, and life experiences. Sharing from personal experience, particularly failures, fosters empathy and makes you more approachable and relatable to others.

Challenge Them

There are some negative associations with the word 'challenge.' However, every now and again, we all need to be challenged, especially if we wish to develop a growth mindset. It is the very essence of it. Find balance while challenging others; don't go too hard, but going too easy will appear patronizing, too. Mention your challenge while reminding everyone to give it their all.

Ask Questions

A good therapist or coach won't instruct their patients. They ask the right questions to help the client better understand themselves, identify the problem, and then make wise decisions. You can follow suit. You can get others to ponder and come up with ideas by posing elegant questions. They'll be grateful for it.

Invest Time in Them

We devote our time to what we enjoy. You may demonstrate to someone how much you value them and your connection with them by giving them your most valuable resource—your time. Spend time cultivating the relationships that make up your life.

Supporting ourselves and others to live our best lives is one of our most important duties. No matter what role we play—parents, spouses, friends, or leaders—it is our responsibility to support people in achieving their full potential.

Conclusion

In today's fast-moving and dynamic world, it's easy to get left behind. Our mindsets are essentially vital for our everyday life, careers, goals, self-confidence, and personal growth. Hence, having a growth mindset is an essential skill to develop.

A growth mindset is having the determination and drive to be adaptable, always learning and taking on tasks without hesitation or fear. Your goal is to 'grow' and develop as a person cognitively and professionally. On the opposing hand, a fixed mindset is geared to holding you back, evoking fear or growth, reluctance to change, and believing that there is a limit to development. We should aim to establish a growth mindset, for ultimate success.

We can achieve this by framing our minds to believing that there is *always* more, taking self-discipline by the reins and using it to enhance our way of thinking, making effective plans for the future and sticking to them, but also remembering that anything can happen, so they should be adaptable, and we should be willing to make the necessary adjustments. Additionally, we should always stay focused on our aspirations, and exercise vigor and determination in everything we do.

And lastly, growth-minded individuals should always view failures and mishaps as ways to improve and grow, learning from them and taking responsibility for our actions. We should be receptive to always learning, and reaching our utmost potential by applying the characteristics of a growth mindset to our lives each day.

The first step is making up your mind. Then, you soar.

Dear reader,

Thank you for reading This book.

I have worked on this project with all my heart and soul. I truly hope that you will benefit from this work. I also hope that you can share this journey of self-improvement with your loved ones and friends.

If you enjoyed it please visit the site where you purchased it and write a brief review. Your feedback is important to me and will help other readers decide whether to read the book too.

Thank you!

May you have a peaceful life.

Wayne Marshall Harrett

Glossary

Advancement: Progression to a higher stage of development.

Contentment: The quality or state of feeling or showing satisfaction with one's possessions, status, or situation.

Curriculum: A set of courses constituting an area of specialization.

Empathy: The action of understanding, being aware of, being sensitive to, and experiencing the feelings, thoughts, and experience of another person of either the past or present without having the feelings, thoughts, and experience fully communicated in an explicit manner.

Entrench: To place (oneself) in a strong defensive position.

Forego: To go before.

Hostile: Having or showing unfriendly feelings.

Innate: Belonging to the essential nature of something.

Intrinsic: Belonging to the essential nature or constitution of a thing.

Hybrid: Something (such as a power plant, vehicle, or electronic circuit) that has two different types of components performing essentially the same function.

Mediocrity: the quality or state of being moderate or low quality, value, ability, or performance.

Misconception: A wrong or inaccurate idea.

Perpetual: Occurring continually: Indefinitely long-continued.

Proficiency: Advancement in knowledge or skill.

Reprimand: To scold or correct usually gently or with kindly intent from a position of authority.

Sustainability: Of, relating to, or being a method of harvesting or using a resource so that the resource is not depleted or permanently damaged.

Theoretical: Existing in a plausible or scientifically acceptable general principle or body of principles offered to explain phenomena.

Vigor: Active bodily or mental strength or force.

References

Adrian, J. (2020, June 21). *Why mindsets matter in relationships.* Medium. https://jonathanoei.medium.com/why-mindset-matters-in-relationships-614c8b98fb99

Alexandra, L. (n.d). *6 Reasons it's okay to fail.* Lifehack. https://www.lifehack.org/articles/productivity/6-reasons-its-okay-fail.html

Angier, M. (n.d). *Top ten ways to help people realize their potential.* Issues I Face. https://issuesiface.com/magazine/help-people-realize-their-potential

Bateman, T. (2012). Masters of the long haul: Pursuing long-term work goals. *Journal of Organizational Behavior,* (33), 984-1006. https://www.researchgate.net/publication/264611161_Masters_of_the_long_haul_Pursuing_long-term_work_goals

Davis, T. (2020, December 3). *What is positive thinking in psychology? 9 Thought-provoking findings.* PositivePsychology.com. https://positivepsychology.com/positive-thinking/#hero-single

Dungy, T. (n.d). *The 7 E's to help others read their potential.* All Pro Dad. https://www.allprodad.com/help-others-reach-full-potential/

Dutton, V. (2015, May 22). *Seven growth mindset habits for success.* Planet Positive Change. https://planetpositivechange.com/seven-growth-mindset-habits-for-success/

Clemson, B. (2020, August 25). 9 Powerful ways to cultivate self-discipline. *Forbes.* https://www.forbes.com/sites/brentgleeson/2020/08/25/8-powerful-ways-to-cultivate-extreme-self-discipline/?sh=68c7d6b2182d

Creative Success. (2021, August 15). *The power of progress: Measure the gain, not the gap.* Omar Itani. https://www.omaritani.com/blog/measure-progress-and-the-gain

Eliam, A. (2019, December 18). *The healing power of acceptance.* Medium. https://medium.com/swlh/the-healing-power-of-acceptance-e75789ce3047

Govil, S. (2020, November 8). *10 Simple ways to keep a happy, healthy mind.* Max Healthcare. https://www.maxhealthcare.in/blogs/10-simple-ways-keep-happy-healthy-mind

Growth mindset. (n.d). Teaching + Lab Learning. https://tll.mit.edu/teaching-resources/inclusive-classroom/growth-mindset/

Guest, L. (2021, July 9). *7 Warning signs that your life is going off track.* Medium. https://medium.com/illumination/7-warning-signs-that-your-life-is-going-off-track-4be601b2bfbb

Hagan, E. (2016, July 11). *Self-regulation vs. self-control.* Psychology today. https://www.psychologytoday.com/us/blog/self-reg/201607/self-regulation-vs-self-control

Hartnell-Young. (2022, July 20). *Overcoming obstacles to a growth mindset.* Skyline. https://skylinefoundation.org.au/overcoming-obstacles-to-a-growth-mindset/

Hasa. (2020, April 23). *Difference Between Constructive and Destructive Criticism.* Pediaa. https://pediaa.com/difference-between-constructive-and-destructive-criticism/#:~:text=The%20main%20difference%20between%20constructive,to%20harm%20or%20insult%20someone.

Healthwise Staff. (2021, June 16). *Dealing with negative thoughts.* Alberta. https://myhealth.alberta.ca/Health/Pages/conditions.aspx?hwid=abl0335

Hill, N. (2014, August 28). *3 Reasons why other people's success should inspire rather than discourage you.* Elite Daily. https://www.elitedaily.com/life/motivation/others-peoples-success-failure

Ho, L. (2022, March 16). *Why you have a fear of failure (and how to overcome it).* Lifehack. https://www.lifehack.org/articles/lifehack/how-fear-of-failure-destroys-success.html

Houston, E. (2019, April 9). *What is goal setting and how to do it well* PositivePsychology.com. https://positivepsychology.com/goal-setting/#hero-single

Indeed Editorial Team. (2020, August 26). *How to practice self-discipline in the workplace.* Indeed. https://in.indeed.com/career-advice/career-development/self-discipline

Indeed Editorial Team. (2021, September 7). *Balancing life between your career and your personal happiness.* Indeed. https://ca.indeed.com/career-advice/career-development/balancing-life#:~:text=Balancing%20your%20life%20allows%20for,being%20distracted%20by%20other%20things.

Indeed Editorial Team. (2021, August 11). *How failures lead to success and lessons that can help you succeed.* Indeed. https://www.indeed.com/career-advice/career-development/failures-lead-to-success

Jonas. (2021, August 18). *10 Characteristics of having a growth mindset.* Jonas Muthoni. https://jonasmuthoni.com/blog/characteristics-of-growth-mindset/

Mangelschots, K. (2019, June 28). *How to find out someone's intentions.* Helathybodyathome. https://healthybodyathome.com/how-to-find-out-someones-intentions/

Mason, T. (n.d). *4 Simple steps to track your progress towards your goals.* Lifehack. https://www.lifehack.org/articles/productivity/4-ways-track-your-progress-toward-your-goals.html

Mayberry, M. (2015, October 6). *Never Stop Growing. Here Are 3 Ways to Maximize Your Potential.* Entrepreneur. https://www.entrepreneur.com/living/never-stop-growing-here-are-3-ways-to-maximize-your/251384

MBO Partners. (2022, May 5). 8 Ways to keep your knowledge and skills current. https://www.mbopartners.com/blog/how-manage-small-business/how-to-keep-your-skills-and-knowledge-current-and-why-it-matters1/

McGuire, M. (2021, April 6). *How to abolish a success scarcity mindset and know there's enough to go around.* Medium. https://medium.com/the-ascent/how-to-abolish-a-success-scarcity-mindset-and-know-theres-enough-to-go-around-26be816a69fe

Mind Tools Content Team. (n.d). *Meeting the standard that matters.* Mind Tools. https://www.mindtools.com/pages/article/professionalism.htm#:~:text=The%20eight%20core%20characteristics%20of,wherever%20you%20find%20yourself%20working.

Moawad, H. (2022, May 27). *Understanding the connection between a growth mindset and neuroplasticity.* Healthine. https://www.healthline.com/health/growth-mindset-neuroplasticity#growth-mindset

Morgan, G. (2014, October 2). *The importance of finding and facing your weaknesses.* Fast Company. https://www.fastcompany.com/3026105/the-importance-of-finding-and-facing-your-weaknesses

Ng, B. (2018). The Neuroscience of Growth Mindset and Intrinsic *Motivation. Brain Sci.* (2), 20. https://www.ncbi.nlm.nih.gov/pmc/articles/PMC5836039/

Obatomi, M. (2022, February 18). *How to give and take constructive criticism.* BetterUp. https://www.betterup.com/blog/how-to-give-and-receive-constructive-criticism-at-work

Own your mistakes. (n.d). Kelly. https://www.kellyservices.ca/ca/careers/career-resource-centre/managing-your-career/own-your-mistakes/

Page, O. (2020, November 4). *How to leave your comfort zone and enter your 'growth zone.'* PositivePsychology.com. https://positivepsychology.com/comfort-zone/

Parincu, Z. (n.d) *Self-Discipline: Definitions, tips & how to develop it.* Well Being Institute. https://www.berkeleywellbeing.com/self-discipline.html

Raypole, C. (2020, June 17). *'Who am I?' How to find your sense of self.* Healthline. https://www.healthline.com/health/sense-of-self#takeaway

Schlegel, R., Hick, J., Ardnt, J., & King, L. (2009). Thine own self: True self-concept accessibility and meaning in life. *National Library of Medicine,* 2, 473-490. https://www.ncbi.nlm.nih.gov/pmc/articles/PMC4714566/

Schramm, D, (n.d). Strategies for dealing with life's difficulties. UtahState University. https://extension.usu.edu/relationships/research/strategies-for-dealing-with-lifes-difficulties

Smith, J. (2022, September 25). *Growth mindset vs fixed mindset: How what you think affects what you achieve.* Mindset Health. https://www.mindsethealth.com/matter/growth-vs-fixed-mindset

Space Coast Daily. (2019, December 19). *Advantages and importance of having a healthy mind and body.* https://spacecoastdaily.com/2019/12/advantages-and-importance-of-having-a-healthy-mind-and-body/#:~:text=People%20with%20good%20physical%20and,vital%20decisions%20or%20to%20relax.

Straw, E. (n.d). *How to effectively turn your weaknesses into strengths.* Success Starts Within. https://www.successstartswithin.com/blog/how-to-effectively-turn-weaknesses-into-strengths

Storoni, M. (2017, September 8). *When low motivation threatens your mission, self-control gets you there.* Inc. Productivity. https://www.inc.com/mithu-storoni/no-motivation-no-problem-as-long-as-you-have-self.html

Tan, S. (2022, February 23). *The growth mindset in relationships.* Elephant Empowering People. https://www.elephant.com.sg/resources/the-growth-mindset-in-relationships/

Thibodeaux, W. (n.d). *4 Ways to protect yourself from manipulative people.* Inc. Life. https://www.inc.com/wanda-thibodeaux/4-ways-to-protect-yourself-from-manipulative-people.html

Tracy, B. (n.d). *6 Reasons setting goals is important.* Brian Tracy International. https://www.briantracy.com/blog/personal-success/importance-of-goal-setting/

Wisdom, K. (2017, May 24). *6 Strategies for coping with change.* Henry Ford Health. https://www.henryford.com/blog/2017/05/coping-with-change

Yvanovich, R. (2021, July 13). *Growth mindset at work: why and how.* TRG. https://blog.trginternational.com/growth-mindset-at-work-why-and-how

Image References

Adrian. (2018, September 3). *No Title.* [Image]. Pixabay. https://pixabay.com/photos/business-success-goals-upwards-3695073/

Altmann, G. (2017, June 23). *No Title.* [Image]. Pixabay. https://pixabay.com/photos/board-school-self-confidence-2433978/

Altmann, G. (2017, June 23). *No Title.* [Image]. Pixabay. https://pixabay.com/photos/board-school-self-confidence-2433984/

Bussinne, S. (2016, September 29). *Hourglass.* [Image]. Pixabay. https://pixabay.com/photos/hourglass-clock-time-deadline-hour-1703330/

Fewings, N. (2022, January 17). *Team Lead Succeed.* [Image]. Unsplash. https://unsplash.com/photos/EkyuhD7uwSM

Grootes, M. (2017, December 12). *Making appointments.* [Image]. Unsplash. https://unsplash.com/photos/flRm0z3MEoA

Hello I'm Nick. (2018, June 11). *Difficult roads lead to beautiful destinations.* [Image]. Unsplash. https://unsplash.com/photos/z1d-LP8sjuI

Inside Weather. (2019, September 6). *Person's feet on table.* [Image]. Unsplash. https://unsplash.com/photos/oDclMzOz31U

Jenson, J. (2018, August 1). *No Title.* [Image]. Unsplash. https://unsplash.com/photos/b3eaH1hguOA

Jordan, B. (2021, May 19). *No Tite.* [Image]. Unsplash. https://unsplash.com/photos/ehKaEaZ5VuU

Jordan, B. (2020, November 24). *No Title.* [Image]. Unsplash. https://unsplash.com/photos/TazDZaDFxaY

Kim, I. (2018, April 9). *Neon sign.* [Image]. Unsplash. https://unsplash.com/photos/gKs6zNil_Ro

Mediamodifer. (2017, December 23). *No Title.* [Image]. Pixabay. https://pixabay.com/photos/plate-food-idea-eat-success-lunch-3033198/

Michaela. (2020, March 17). *A book.* [Image]. Pixabay. https://pixabay.com/photos/a-book-pages-read-training-novel-5178205/

Overgoor, R. (2021, January 23). *Goals.* [Image]. Unsplash. https://unsplash.com/photos/EdKCckXXRCI

Perkins, J. (2017, May 7). *Reach.* [Image]. Unsplash. https://unsplash.com/photos/7FOSJVtUtac

Rae, S. (2017, October 10). *No Title*. [Image]. Unsplash. https://unsplash.com/photos/geM5lzDj4Iw

Schaferle. (2017, May 5). *No Title*. [image]. Pixabay. https://pixabay.com/photos/battle-boxing-unfair-weak-strong-2284723/

Schneider, I. (2016, February 18). *Two persons standing on gray tile*. [Image]. Unsplash. https://unsplash.com/photos/TamMbr4okv4

Thought Catalog. (2018, October 18). *The Strength In Our Scars*. [Image]. Unsplash. https://unsplash.com/photos/o38AW4xnwEo

www.ingramcontent.com/pod-product-compliance
Lightning Source LLC
Chambersburg PA
CBHW021715110125
20180CB00044B/515